BLACKJACK BLUEBOOK

II

the Simplest Winning Strategies ever published

FRED RENZEY

BLACKJACK BLUEBOOK II
the Simplest Winning Strategies ever published

Publisher: BLACKJACK MENTOR PRESS

Send Inquiries to: BLACKJACK MENTOR
P.O Box 92283, Elk Grove Village, IL 60009 - 2283

ISBN# 0-692-83948-8
       978-0-692-83948-5

ELEVENTH PRINTING
2021
(Note that pages 25, 47, 64.1, 64.2, 71, 71.1, 71.2, 81.1, 81.2, 82, 87.1, 87.2, 89, 91, 99, 99.1, 99.2, 102, 103, 117, 119, 124, 128, 129, 154, 155, 157, 158, 161, 174, 176, 177, 178, 179, 182, 183 183.1 and 183.2 of this eleventh printing contain updated or extra information which did not appear in the 2006 printing).

Printed in U.S.A.
The material contained in this book is intended to educate and inform the reader. It is further cautioned that gambling is an uncertain venture carrying a broad range of financial consequences.

THIS BOOK IN A NUTSHELL

Let's cut right through all the nonsense. You and I both know that at least 99% of the blackjack players are losers in the long run. Yet, there *are* people who turn in a winning year most of the time. So just what does a winner do right that all the other losers don't?

The chief difference lies in how winning gamblers and losing gamblers *think* when they play blackjack. Losers are *fixated* on money management, the flow of the cards and the influence of somebody else's play upon their own chances. There's no room for those fables in a winner's game plan. The first thing this book will do is expose and rid you of *senseless preoccupations* that get in the way of winning.

Another entire chapter is dedicated to improving your game *beyond* basic strategy without jumping over into card counting. Several *valid* techniques are illustrated in *vivid* detail, which scarcely appear *anywhere* in print.

And finally, it's been well documented in so many blackjack books over the years that to actually beat the game, you have to count cards. Basically, this is *true*. But you no longer have to become that *Pentium android* who calculates higher mathematics at the speed of light. What you *do* need to have though, is an *awareness* of at least *some* of the key cards that have been played. Inside you'll find surprisingly easy ways to "spot case" a shoe and recognize when the odds of the game have switched around to favor *you*.

It took 18 billion computer generated blackjack hands to develop and fine tune the strategies in this book. A prime requirement was that they all run silky smooth at the table.

I've made no earth shattering discoveries related to gaining the edge at blackjack. What I have done is *dissect, simplify* and *build upon* the timeless concepts that broke the game open in the 1960's. In their 21st century down-to-earth form, just about any avid player can put them to effective use.

ACKNOWLEDGMENTS

Cover photo by Emil Schiavo

Cover design by Dorothy Kavka

Proof reading by Emily Mendoza and Stan Weiss

Special Acknowledgment to
Stanford Wong

and his *"Blackjack Count Analyzer"*. The blackjack strategies developed for this book consumed roughly 11 billion computer simulated hands. Although I have several pieces of analytical blackjack software, I find Wong's *BCA* the most adaptable to custom situations. It has improved my understanding of blackjack's finer points immensely.

TABLE of CONTENTS

WHAT'S YOUR BLACKJACK I. Q.?

So you like to play casino blackjack. Think you know the game pretty well? Of course you do. I've never met a blackjack player who figured he was a bad one. Well, before you get into this book, *we'd better find out how much you really understand about casino "21"*.

Following is a fifteen question blackjack "I. Q." test. It's multiple choice. It's not super-technical, but it does quiz you on more than just the basic strategy. If that's all it was, you could get a perfect score on it by simply memorizing a chart. But would that mean you truly know the game? Not at all! There's a lot to be aware of at the blackjack table besides your basic hitting, standing and doubling down. Yet ironically, most players exhaust their energy paying attention to things that don't even matter -- and are oblivious to the stuff that counts.

Go ahead, take the quiz. I think you'll find it both interesting and eye opening. It starts out with some very simple basics and progresses on from there. The answers are provided at the end along with detailed explanations and scoring. You may find that you don't know as much about casino "21" as you thought, *and that's probably costing you money*. In that case, keep right on going and read the rest of this book. It will probably make you a much better blackjack player.

**IT COULD EVEN TURN YOU
INTO A LIFETIME WINNER!**

Blackjack I/Q Quiz

1) A "soft" hand is:
    a) a hand containing an Ace counted as 11.
    b) a hand containing an Ace counted as 1.
    c) a hand with a total of 11 or less.

2) Third base is:
    a) the seat just next to the dealer's shoe.
    b) the third player to act in the hand.
    c) the seat just next to the discard tray.

3) The dealer will have a 10 in the hole:
    a) just about 30% of the time.
    b) just about half the time.
    c) just about 70% of the time.

4) When the dealer has a 5 up, she will break;
    a) 3 times out of 7
    b) 4 times out of 7
    c) 5 times out of 7
    d) 6 times out of 7

5) It's the first hand of a full six deck shoe with 6 players. You have *Ace/9* for a *20* against the dealer's *Ace* up. Among all 13 cards on board, there are no *10s*. What's your play?
    a) take Insurance regardless of what hand you have.
    b) decline Insurance regardless of what hand you have.
    c) take Insurance for ¼ of your bet.
    d) take Insurance if you have 19 or higher.

6) Which of these hands are you most likely to win?
    a) 20 against a deuce up.
    b) 20 against a 4 up.
    c) 20 against a 6 up.
    d) 20 against an 8 up.

7) All four hands below should be hit. With three of them, standing would be only a small to moderate mistake, but standing with the other is a major error. Name the hand.
    a) 16 against a 7 up.
    b) 16 against a 10 up.
    c) 12 against a 2 up.
    d) 12 against a 3 up.

8) You've just made a very large bet. Being dealt 11 against the dealer's 3, you double down and catch an Ace. The player at third base has 12. How do you want him to play his hand so as to maximize your own chances of winning?

> *a) stand and save the bust card for the dealer.*
> *b) you couldn't care less.*
> *c) hit since that would be proper basic strategy.*

9) You and the fellow at third base are playing alone and things are going well. Suddenly, a new player appears at first base and plops down a bet. Realizing that this will change the flow of the cards, you should:

> *a) pull your bet back and wait 'till the shuffle.*
> *b) play only at "no mid-shoe entry" tables to preserve the order of the cards.*
> *c) just accept the cards that Lady Luck deals you.*

10) When you have an Ace/7 against a 6 up, odds are you'll win 16 times out of 25 if you stand -- and 15 out of 25 whether you hit or double down. Therefore, you should:

> *a) stand.*
> *b) hit.*
> *c) double down.*

11) You're playing alone against the dealer. Your first hand off the top of a six deck shoe is 2/5/5/4 against the dealer's 10 showing. Your correct play is to:

> *a) stand.*
> *b) hit*

12) A pair of 8's against the dealer's 10 up should be split because:

> *a) it gives you the edge on the two hands combined.*
> *b) it loses less than not splitting.*
> *c) it turns a losing situation into a "break even" proposition.*

13) A player next to you has a pair of 7's against the dealer's 3 up. Being out of chips, he asks if you'd like to put up the money and take one of his 7's. Should you do it?

> *a) no, since it's most likely a bad deal if he's offering it to you.*
> *b) yes, since splitting 7/7 against a 3 is proper basic strategy.*

3

14) You're playing two spots and have been dealt a 17 on one hand and a blackjack on the other. The dealer has has an Ace up. Your correct decisions are to:

a) take even money on blackjack and decline Insurance on 17.
b) take Insurance on 17 and just gamble with your blackjack.
c) refuse both Insurance and even money.
d) take both Insurance and even money.

15) You're watching a six deck game from the aisle. On the first hand of the shoe the dealer has a 3 up. First base splits a pair of 6's, then finally stands with 13 and 14 after taking two hits to each 6. The next man doubles down with 9 but catches a baby. The rookie at third base then splits a pair of 5's, catches a 7 on each and doubles down with both 12's! The dealer promptly makes a five card 21 and the entire table empties out except for the rookie at third base. What's your move?

a) run from that table and the moron at third base.
b) step right up and play two hands at a time.
c) wait 'till third base leaves, then take his seat.
d) watch the next few hands to see how the dealer's running.

ANSWERS

1) **A:** a soft hand is one that contains an *Ace* counted as *11*. If the next hit brings your total over *21*, then the value of the *Ace* can can be reverted to *"1"* -- hence the term *"soft"*.
(score 1 point)

2) **C:** the last seat to act before the dealer is referred to as "third base". It's right next to the discard tray.
(score 1 point)

3) **A:** Since roughly 30% of the cards are *10's*, that's how often the dealer will have one in the hole. It's also how often the next card will be a *10*. Playing your hands as though the dealer has a *10* in the hole is a strategy littered with costly flaws.
(score 2 points)

4) **A:** Contrary to popular blackjack folklore, there is no up-card with which the dealer will break more often than not. She'll make a hand 4 times out of 7 when showing a *5* or a *6*, and things just get tougher against every other up-card. Thus, no dealer's up-card is truly a so-called "bust card".
(score 2 points)

5) **B:** Do *not* take Insurance! Even with 13 *"no-tens"* on the table, there's still only a 32% chance that the dealer has blackjack! Right off the top of the shoe, you'd need 25 straight *no-tens* to make Insurance the right play — regardless of your hand.
(score 2 points)

6) **D:** When you have *20* vs. an *8* up, as an 8-to-1 favorite you have the strongest hand you can be dealt that you could still possibly lose. With the dealer's tendency to have a made *18*, plus the times she'll already have *17* or *19* by turning over a *9* or *Ace* in the hole, there are very few draws she will ever make to beat your *20*. With the other three hands, you are between a 4-to1 and 6-to-1 favorite on each.
(score 1 point)

7) **A:** *16* vs. a *7* up is the hand most likely to be converted from a loser into a winner the times you hit and don't bust. Notice the difference between catching say, a *deuce* to your *16* against a *7* up, rather than against a *10*. Against the *7* up, you're probably going to win and against the *10*, you'll still probably lose. It's a foolish, *rookie* mistake to ever stand with *16* against a *7!*
(score 3 points)

8) **B:** Just ask yourself which of the next two cards is more likely to break the dealer. Third base's *own* chances would improve by taking one blind hit to his *12*. But it's 50-50 whether the *dealer* will do better with that *very next card* – or the one *after* it. *Your* odds to win remain the same no matter what third base does.
(score 3 points)

9) **C:** Was your lucky run about to end or about to continue? Now you'll be receiving third base's original card rather than your own. It shouldn't be any worse for you than it would've been

for him. In fact, if the dealer let you choose any two cards from the next six -- without being fully aware of their order you wouldn't know which ones to pick! Forget the voo-doo stuff. *(score 3 points)*

10) **C: Double down!** Winning 15 hands out of 25 for $20 each makes more money than winning 16 out of 25 for $10 each! There are numerous situations in blackjack where the most likely way to win the hand is not the most profitable overall play. *(score 2 points)*

11) **A: Stand!** The basic strategy says to hit with a starting hand of *16* against a *10*. But *2/5/5/4* is no starting hand! Few players realize this hand is such a borderline decision that the presence of any *4's* or *5's* in your *16* make standing the better play. *(score 4 points)*

12) **B:** Over time, *16* against a *10* actually loses more than twice as much money as *8* against a *10*. So your thriftiest decision is to create two *8's* and lose less money as time goes by. *(score 2 points)*

13) **A:** Splitting two *7's* against a *3* is proper basic strategy because it too, loses less than playing a *14*. But the hand is still a loser! As a mere bystander, you have no loss to reduce, so just stay out of this one. *(score 2 points)*

14) **C:** If like most players you chose "A", believe it or not, you'll get exactly the same combined result as if you'd chosen "B"! This is true regardless of what the dealer has or makes. Run through the possible scenarios and you'll see. Choice "C" however, will bring a better long term result than both "A" and "B" *(score 3 points)*.

15) **B:** When the dealer makes a clutch *21*, players tend to back off, fearing that he's "hot". Likewise, if a player makes a "bonehead" move, most others become afraid to play with him. *All nonsense!* What's *not* nonsense is that a barrage of small cards have just come out, and the players are going to have an edge for at least the next couple of hands. *Get in there!* *(score 4 points)*.

IF YOU SCORED:

0 - 10 points: *go back to playing the lotto!*

11 - 15 points: *a little bit of knowledge is a dangerous thing; for you!*

16 - 23 points: *you have an average understanding of the game of blackjack; a typical overall contributor to casino profits.*

24 - 29 points: *you're a fairly solid player and make your wins here and there.*

30 - 35 points: *you're far above the norm and probably give the house a serious run for its money on a consistent basis.*

Summary: Please don't feel intimidated or offended if you scored poorly. The truth is, the average blackjack player has no idea how far off base most of his game plan is. That's what this book is for. So get into it, *absorb* and *digest.*

SECTION A

the Unique Nature of Blackjack

1

Why Blackjack?

Of all the casino games on the floor, why gamble your money on blackjack? After all, what would make *"21"* different from any other casino-banked game?

First off, you need to remember that casino games are the product of a business that was created to make money for its owners. In theory, these games were intended to be mathematically impenetrable over the long haul. You're not really supposed to have a shot at beating the house once everything evens out. The casino can best achieve this "unbeatable" status through games of chance that involve the element of "replacement", such as craps or roulette.

"Replacement" means that when a roulette wheel is spun, if number *23* comes up, that number is *not* wiped off the wheel for the next spin. Likewise, when the number *6* is rolled with a pair of dice, all the faces that add up to *6* also remain intact for the next roll. It would be like dealing the *Ace* of spades, then shuffling it back into the deck before dealing the next card. Consequently, numbers *23* and *6* are just as likely to come up again on the next try as they were just before. This replacement feature makes craps

9

and roulette games of *"independent events"*. Since there's no process of elimination, no number is ever "due". So the odds never change for the next spin of the wheel or roll of the dice.

With this knowledge in their pockets, in order to gain the upper hand, the house only has to pay you odds that are a bit shorter than those *constant* odds against that number coming up. Here's a basic example.

Since there are 38 numbers on an American roulette wheel, the odds against number *23* being spun *(or any other number)* are 37 to 1. And the payoff odds for picking a single number are 35 to 1. Betting just one number, after 38 *averaged* spins of the wheel you'll have 37 losers and one winner. By offering only 35 to 1 payoff odds, the house knows it will have a 2 slot edge on you at *all* times. This 2 slot difference between your payoff odds and the odds against hitting your number becomes the reason why the house wins and the players lose in the long run.   And it's all because of something called.........

The BASIC PRINCIPLE of PROFITABLE GAMBLING

You see, for every dollar lost in gambling there is a dollar won. Right now as you're reading this, somewhere in the world two people are betting on something. Most likely, somebody has the edge while the other person is at a disadvantage. The *Basic Principle of Profitable Gambling* is what determines who's who. In short, the principle states that:

**IN ORDER TO GAIN THE EDGE ON A BET,
YOUR PAYOFF ODDS MUST BE HIGHER
THAN YOUR ODDS AGAINST WINNING IT**

Suppose I were to set a deck of cards on the table, then challenge you to cut the deck and name the suit of the card you were going to cut. If I offered you even money, let's say my $1 against your $1 would you take that bet? Of course you wouldn't! You'd refuse it because it's easy to see that you'll lose a buck more often than you'll win one.

But what if I offered $10 to your $1? Now you should

10

certainly bet me! That's because even though you'll usually lose, you'll more than make up for it the times you win. How do you know? With four suits in a deck of cards, you have three ways to lose and one way to win. That makes odds of 3-to-1 against winning your bet. Over time, you will in fact lose your bet three times for each winner you make.

Now, what would happen if you were paid say, $3 each time you picked the right suit and lost $1 every time you were wrong? You'd break even wouldn't you? So when your payoff odds are *equal* to the odds against winning your bet, you have an *even gamble*. If your payoff odds are higher, you have the edge. And if they're lower, you're at a disadvantage and are destined to lose over time. *That's the Basic Principle of Profitable Gambling.*

Every wagering proposition in casino games of independent events is based on this "short payoff" principle. When you're getting even money to bet "red" at roulette, you have 18 reds to win with, and 18 blacks -- plus 2 greens that beat you. That's 20 to 18 against you! If you bet black, you have the same deal. They've got you coming and going! Even on the ever-popular pass line at craps, the odds to win even money are *always* 251 to 244 against the player. In every case you're on the short end of the *Basic Principle of Profitable Gambling.* And as difficult as it may be to accept, there is *no way* to overcome this by following trends or streaks, since the wheel and the dice have no memory whatsoever. Yes, streaks do occur, but you cannot predict the arrival of one. And once you've established that you're in a streak, it's been demonstrated over and over that it's just as likely to reverse itself *right now* as continue. Also, no matter what you may be inclined to believe, there is no *"accountant in the sky"* forcing short term results to *"even out"* when they become unbalanced. That's because:

LOP-SIDED RESULTS ARE NOT CORRECTED; THEY MERELY FADE INTO THE PAST

Remember that last statement. It's one of the most important things you'll ever learn about gambling. The house is so certain of this that many casinos are cordial enough to post an electronic tote

11

board displaying the last 15 or 20 roulette numbers to come up. At the mini-baccarat table, they provide pre-printed forms and pencils for you to track dealer and player streaks. Is the house giving you information to beat them with? Hardly! In effect, they are telling you, *"Go ahead and chart all the past results you want"*. They know it doesn't make any difference -- *and so should you!*

Also in roulette, craps and even baccarat, once you put your money down there's absolutely no way to influence the outcome of your bet. You have nothing to do now but wait for the result. At this point, they are games of *pure* chance. With these factors working for them, the house has a truly *bulletproof* gambling arrangement. They simply have you betting the shorter end of the stick! Short term fluctuations will literally force the player to win some of the time. Eventually though, the law of large numbers must be adhered to and the casino will come out on top.

The *UNIQUE NATURE* of BLACKJACK

Blackjack is different from this in two very important ways. First, it's one of the few casino games in which the player uses his judgment to make decisions *after* his bet has been placed. These decisions will either increase or decrease his chances of winning the bet. For example, if you always stand when you have *2-4-Ace* against a dealer's *4* up, you'll win only 46% of those hands, but if you hit you'll win 53% of them. Hence, for you blackjack may be the best game in the house, or be "just not your game" depending upon how well you make your decisions.

It's true that some of the newer table games like *Mississippi Stud* or *3-Card Poker* also offer the player the opportunity to make strategic playing decisions. But these games are modern day inventions, painstakingly developed according to a very exacting set of mathematical probabilities. The house advantage using *perfect* basic strategy with these is 1½% to 2½% — but the players' misguided poker instincts usually leave them closer to 4% behind the 8-ball.

On the other hand, the game of blackjack is well over a century old. When its rules were first structured, putting the house at an advantage was much more complicated than just paying

35-to-1 on a 37-to-1 shot. The game's developers had no computers to determine what the exact percentages would be in many of the more extreme nuances that can arise. But that was okay because the player too, would be limited by his own reasoning powers. That being the case, the available design tools of their day were sufficient to provide the house with a comfortable edge over any human of that era. And so it went for several decades. Then came the age of computers.

Today's computer derived playing strategies for blackjack extend well beyond the players' own perceptive logic. In a casino gambling arena, where house advantages on table games average about 3%, a well-informed blackjack player gives up just a $1/2\%$ edge to the house in a typical multi-deck game by doing nothing more than memorizing a basic strategy chart. A $1/2\%$ disadvantage means playing 200 hands and finishing one bet behind if the odds run perfectly true to form. You can be pretty sure it was never intended to be that close of a contest.

The second big difference about blackjack is, unlike craps and roulette, it is a game of "dependent" events. That means once you've been dealt a *4* and a *3,* then hit it with a *deuce, 5* and a *6* for example, those cards go into the discard rack and *cannot* be dealt again for the remainder of the shoe. As the cards grow more and more depleted, sometimes certain hands become easier to make and certain other hands grow more scarce. In fact;

THERE ARE TIMES WHEN YOUR CHANCES OF BEING DEALT A BLACKJACK ARE 1 in 17, AND OTHER TIMES WHEN THEY ARE 1 in 25

This kind of thing *never* happens in craps, roulette or Caribbean stud. It's like knowing that the number *10* in craps now has one chance in *nine* of coming up rather than the normal one chance in *twelve*. These things do happen repeatedly in blackjack, and can make your odds against winning that next hand shorter than your payoff odds. *That's what can put you on the right side of the Basic Principle of Profitable Gambling.* Of all the house-banked casino games, those are the reasons why you would choose to gamble your money on blackjack.

Chapter 1
KEY POINTS

1) For every dollar lost in gambling, somebody wins a dollar. And in nearly every gambling proposition, somebody has the upper hand.

2) The casino strives to market products with the edge on their side. This is most easily accomplished by offering games of "independent" events like craps or roulette.

3) With most casino games you make very few or no decisions after you've placed your bet. In blackjack, your decisions greatly affect the outcome of your wager.

4) In most other casino games, the odds never vary from one bet to the next. In blackjack the odds keep shifting with the removal of every next card.

5) Because of numbers 3 and 4, the odds against winning your next hand are sometimes lower than your payoff odds. This can put you on the right side of the *Basic Principle of Profitable Gambling.*

6) Very, very few casino games can be beaten at all -- long term. Of the few that can, blackjack is the most readily beatable.

2

the House Edge

Before you can intelligently attempt to beat the casino at blackjack, you have to realize where their edge comes from in the first place. In this game, you're not just betting with 18 ways to win and 20 ways to lose the way you are with *"red"* in roulette.

No, blackjack is not that simple, and it's not that absolute. There are thousands upon thousands of variables involved. Still and all at first blush though, things seem pretty even. I mean, you're trying to make *21* and the dealer's trying to make *21*. You draw cards and the dealer draws cards. If you both get *18*, it's a "push". What could be fairer than that?

Well, things would be a lot fairer if you could get a "push" on *22*; or on *26*! But that's not how it is. You see;

THE HOUSE DRAWS ITS EDGE FROM THE
FACT THAT THE PLAYER MUST ACT FIRST

This is the casino's *sole* advantage in blackjack. Because of this, if the player breaks, the house wins right now -- even if the dealer would have busted had he been forced to play out his own hand! If the player decided to play his hands the same way the dealer plays his, simultaneous busts would occur 8% of the time. There's the casino's initial edge.

So, what can you do about that? If you decide to counteract it by never busting yourself, the dealer will make more "*17* or better" hands than you will -- sort of a catch "22". *It's impossible to compensate for having to act first, when the first one to break automatically loses.* All else being equal, acting first is a *huge* disadvantage; an 8% disadvantage!

But alas, all else is *not* equal. Apparently realizing that this would be too big an edge for the house, the developers of the game decided to give some "perks" to the player that the dealer doesn't get. The following table outlines the differences in the rules between the player and the dealer, then defines where the advantage lies for each difference.

WHO HAS THE ADVANTAGE?

PLAYER	DEALER	ADVANTAGE
acts first	acts last	dealer
3-to-2 on blackjack	even money	player
hit/stand at will	must hit 16/stand 17	player
may double down	no doubling	player
may split pairs	no splitting	player

As it turns out, blackjack is a game with considerably uneven rules. Notice that except for having to act first, every difference in the rules favors the player. Also, because the dealer must follow rigid rules and plays the game like a robot, every dealer is just as *tough* as any other. So then, the edge the house may have against any given player is ultimately determined by how well that player uses his options.

Starting with an initial house edge of about 8% then, the player begins to peck away at his disadvantage by using his options the best way he knows how. The next table will tell you in round numbers, how much you can knock off that house edge by playing your cards right.

16

MAXIMIZING *the* PLAYER'S OPTIONS

3-to-2 bonus for blackjack	**regain 2¹/₄%**
Proper hitting/standing	**regain 3¹/₄%**
Proper doubling down	**regain 1¹/₂%**
Proper pair splitting	**regain ¹/₂%**

The first thing you'll notice from the table is that the 3-to-2 payoff for the player's blackjacks will eat into that basic 8% dealer's edge by about 2¹/₄%. This one's a no-brainer; you can't mess it up. But you'd better use your head with the remaining three options, or they'll just turn out to be more rope for you to hang yourself with.

As the table illustrates, if you can simply learn to hit, stand, double down and split properly, you'll reduce the casino's mathematical advantage down to roughly ¹/₂% in a multi-deck shoe game with typical blackjack rules. With one or two decks, the player's disadvantage might be a few tenths percent smaller, and with tighter rules it would be a tad larger.

That kind of house edge is ten times smaller than at roulette and five times smaller than Caribbean stud. In fact, it's small enough that if you did nothing more than play all your hands right, you should win 7 playing sessions for every 8 losing days you have. And that's without keeping track of any of the cards. It's very tough to cut that close a gamble anywhere else on the casino floor.

The other day I was at the blackjack table with a dealer who stated flatly that she never gambles. I asked her if she carries collision insurance on her automobile. *"Sure!"*, she replied. *"Well there you go!"*, I said. *"You're betting that you're going to smash up your car and if you don't -- you lose!"* Furthermore, I'm sure she wasn't getting good enough odds on her premium to make it a profitable bet.

You see, for insurance companies to remain solvent they need to collect more money in premiums than they pay out in damage claims. That puts the policyholders on the short end of that ever important *Basic Principle of Profitable Gambling*. The

17

sharpies who figure out what kind of odds they're going to lay you are called "actuaries". The insurance companies are the "bookies". Problem is, that's a bet most people just can't afford *not* to make! So in that scenario, we give our insurance companies the house edge and carry the protection necessary to guard against disaster.

But in blackjack, with enough expertise you don't have to give house an edge. It's actually possible to turn the mathematical tables on them by a very small, but valuable margin. That part comes four or five chapters later on in this book. For now, let's briskly move through the basics.

Chapter 2
KEY POINTS

1) The mathematical innards of blackjack are much more complex than most other casino games.

2) The player and dealer each abide by their own sets of rules and restrictions.

3) The house gains its sole edge in blackjack by forcing the player to act first.

4) Every other rule difference favors the player.

5) Using his strategy options, the player can improve or worsen his chances to win, making blackjack a game of skill.

6) If the player can just play all his hands correctly, he can nearly eliminate the house edge altogether

3

Rules of the Game

Blackjack is the most popular table game in the casino. And since you've purchased a book that was written primarily for the serious player, you probably already know exactly how it's played. But just in case you're a "newbie", I'll provide a basic outline of the rules and procedures for casino *"21"* on the next few pages. If you're an experienced journeyman, you might want to skip right to Chapter 4.

Casino blackjack is played on a semi-circular table that usually seats seven players, but there's nothing sacred about the number of gamblers at a *"21"* table. Several casinos also provide some slightly smaller tables with only five betting spots in certain pits. The largest blackjack table I've ever seen was at the *Four Queens Casino* in Las Vegas. That seated twelve players and required two dealers. A more typical blackjack layout is shown in the illustration on the following page. Pay close attention to the fine print on the playing surface. It doesn't always read identically in every casino.

19

Typical
Blackjack Layout

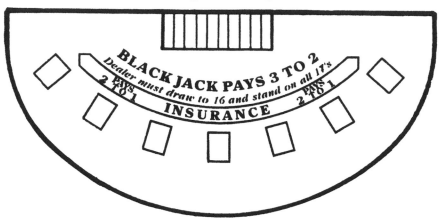

The dealer stands on the flat side of the table and the players sit around the circular portion. These days, the dealer usually deals the game from a *"shoe"* containing anywhere from four to eight decks of cards. But in some places, the game is still dealt with just one or two decks held in the dealer's hand. When *"21"* is played with a shoe, all the players' cards are usually dealt face-up. When it's dealt from the hand, the players cards normally come face-down.

These two separate dealing procedures call for different ways to tell the dealer how you wish to play your cards. In the old days, all the games were dealt face-down from the dealer's hand. This style has come to be known as a "pitch game". The player would pick up his cards and scratch with them towards himself on the felt if he wanted another card. If he wished to stand, he would slide his cards face-down underneath his chips.

As the years went by, more and more casinos went to the multi-deck shoe games in an effort to protect themselves from card counters, cheats and to speed up the game. In a face-up shoe game, the players are ***not allowed to touch the cards***. To take a hit you must tap on the table in front of your hand. If you wish to stand, you must wave the dealer off by passing your hand over your cards.

Notice that in neither case are you required, or even encouraged to speak to the dealer. This is largely because the *"eye in the sky"* wants to be able to oversee the game with a crystal clear understanding of what's going on.

Dealer's Rules

The dealer's rules in blackjack are simple. He has no options and might as well be a robot. If he has less than *17*, he *must* take a card. If he has *17* or more, he *cannot* take any cards. If, in taking more cards the dealer goes over *21*, he automatically loses to any player who is still in the hand. The only sticky part is when the dealer turns up a hand like the one pictured below:

This is called a *"soft 17"* because an *Ace* may be counted as *1* or *11* in blackjack. Many players call this hand "*7 or 17*". But each casino decides to call it either one or the other when it's in the dealer's hand. If the printing on the table reads, ***"Dealer must stand on all 17's"***, then he must stand when he turns up an *Ace/6*, and his hand is finished at *17*. If the table printing reads, ***"Dealer must Hit soft 17"***, then his *Ace/6* is regarded as *7* and he must hit it. The same principle applies if the dealer turns up an *Ace/2*, hits it and catches a *4*. This is still a *soft 17* and falls under the same set of rules.

The funny thing is, if the dealer hits his *Ace/6* and catches an *Ace*, he doesn't have *8,* but *18* and now must stand. As you might guess from the sound of all this, hitting a *soft 17* is to the dealer's advantage. *You'd prefer to play in a casino where the dealer stands on all 17's.* All other rules being equal, the dealer hitting a *soft 17* will increase the house edge by $^{2}/_{10}$%.

21

Player's Options

The player has at least four options that the dealer doesn't have. They are listed below.

Hit/Stand: The player may always stand or hit as he sees fit. If he goes over *21* while taking a card, he automatically and immediately loses. It doesn't matter if the dealer goes over *21* afterwards. As soon as the player busts, his chips are raked in, and he's out of the hand.

Double Down: Sometimes the player is dealt two starting cards that are not a complete hand, but have good potential to make a powerful hand with one more card. A classic example of such a hand is shown next.

An initial hand of *11* is a powerful start because 30% of all the cards are *10's (10's, Jacks, Queens and Kings)*. Thus, the next card will make *21* almost a third of the time. Even an *8* or a *9* will make *19* or *20* respectively -- all good hands.

On his first two cards, if the player thinks he has the advantage over the dealer, he may double his bet and take one more card. The conditional trade-off for being permitted to increase his bet *after* seeing his cards is; one hit is *all* the player can take! If he catches a *deuce* on his *11*, he's stuck with *13*. Nevertheless, doubling down is a boon to the player in the right spots.

In most casinos, the player can double down with any two starting cards. This would include hands like *Ace/4*, or *5/3*. But a few houses limit your doubling down to certain hands, such as totals of *9, 10* and *11* only. It's better for the skilled player if he can double on any two card holding.

Splitting Pairs: Anytime the player is dealt a pair on his starting hand, he may opt to split them into two separate hands of one card each, and play them out individually if he thinks that's the better way to go. When doing this he will have two bets riding, each one the size of the original wager. A classic example of a good splitting hand would be:

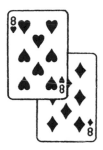

A pair of *8's* is such an excellent hand to split because it breaks up a *16* -- the worst hand you can get. You'll learn later on in this book that a pair of *8's* should virtually always be split. If you do split your pair and receive a third card of the same rank, most casinos allow you to "re-split" by creating a third new hand. Four hands is usually the maximum that can be created by splitting and re-splitting pairs.

Insurance: Every time the dealer's up-card is an *Ace*, he is apt to have blackjack. All it takes is a *10-card* in the hole. If the *10* is there, he's an automatic winner unless you have blackjack yourself, which ties. So whenever the dealer has an *Ace* showing, he will ask the players if they want *"Insurance"*.

Insurance is a side bet you can make, separate from the wager on your hand that the dealer does in fact have a *10* in the hole for a blackjack. That's right -- if the dealer has blackjack you *win* the side bet, and if he doesn't, you *lose*. Hence, the term, "Insurance". It's a hedge bet.

The price of Insurance is half the amount the player has riding on the hand -- and it offers 2-to-1 payoff odds if it wins. That price combined with those odds will typically break you even on the hand if you take Insurance and the dealer has blackjack. Here's how. Let's say you've bet $10 on your hand and were dealt:

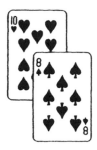

The dealer has an *Ace* showing, so you ante up another $5 by placing it in the Insurance ring right in front of your bet. The dealer looks at her hole card, and turns up the *10* of clubs for a blackjack. Now the situation looks like this:

YOUR HAND   **DEALER'S HAND**

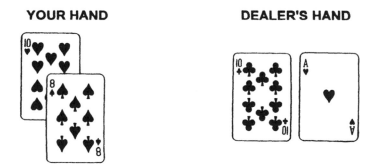

The dealer's *21* beats your *18*, so you lose $10 on your hand. But you've won the $5 Insurance bet at 2-to-1 payoff odds, collecting $10 there. All in all, you break even. The same thing would happen if you had *7* or *12* instead of *18*.

There is one other case however, in which you don't break even. It's when you've been dealt a blackjack yourself. Now, if the dealer has the *10* in the hole underneath her *Ace* and you've taken Insurance, things look like this:

YOUR HAND   **DEALER'S HAND**

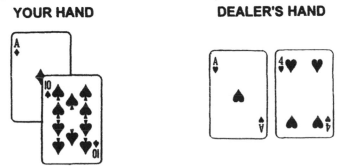

Your hands tie and no money is exchanged there. But you still win the $5 insurance wager receiving 2-to-1 odds, thereby netting a $10 profit. But what if the dealer doesn't have blackjack? Let's take a look:

YOUR HAND   **DEALER'S HAND**

Now you beat the dealer and get paid 3-to-2, or $15 for your blackjack. But you lose the $5 Insurance bet, once again netting $10 on the dual transaction! So whenever the you have blackjack and the dealer has an *Ace* up, if you simply ask the dealer for *"even money"*, she'll pay you before she even checks her hole card for a blackjack. It's no wonder that nine out of ten blackjack players make this play every time. It's a sure thing! However, in Chapter 5, we'll learn why it's the *wrong* play!

Surrender: This fairly uncommon option is probably offered in only 15% to 20% of the casinos in the country, but is worth mentioning for its strategic value. On your first two cards, providing the dealer doesn't have blackjack, you may give up *half* your bet and get out of the hand if you don't like your chances. A classic surrender hand would be the player's *16* against a dealer's *10* up. You would take the surrender option any time you think that losing half your bet is a better deal than having to play the hand out. In Chapter 5, we'll learn that there are indeed a handful of situations that should be surrendered if the option is available. And the more skilled you are, there more valuable "surrender" is.

Many other "specialty" rules are occasionally in force at various casinos, but most don't affect the game appreciably. Here, you've been given a "nutshell" summary of how standard blackjack is played in gambling houses throughout the U.S.A. and most casinos abroad. In Chapter 5, *(the Basic Strategy)*, you'll learn how to take proper advantage of those rules.

Chapter 3
KEY POINTS

1) Two basically different styles of blackjack are played in the casinos; single or double deck "pitch" games dealt from the dealer's hand -- and four to eight deck "shoe" games. The shoe games outnumber hand held blackjack by about a 10 to 1 ratio.

2) All else being equal, the fewer the decks used, the better the percentages are for the player – even if he doesn't keep track of the cards.

3) In some casinos the dealer must stand on all 17's, and in others he must hit a "soft" 17. It's moderately better for the player if the dealer stands with this hand.

4) The options the player may use to manage his hands are hitting, standing, doubling down, splitting, taking Insurance and in some casinos, surrendering.

5) Most poor players think the *surrender* option is a sucker play, but good players understand that it can be used to their advantage.

SECTION B

What Makes Blackjack Tick?

4

Blackjack Myths

Paying attention to important things that happen at the blackjack table can definitely help you win, but *they have to be the right things.* Problem is, the average player focuses intently on a lot of nonsense that can't really help at all. Gambling does funny things to people. So many well-rounded individuals who run their lives in a deliberate and logical fashion become illogical and downright superstitious when it comes to gambling.

Now, I know that no gambler wants to be called superstitious, so let's replace the word "superstition" with "myth". It's ironic that myths are what bring many people to gambling in the first place, when these myths can be the very things that'll keep them from winning at it. If you're preoccupied with myths when you gamble, it'll govern your behavior in an unproductive, and sometimes downright self-destructive way.

Gambling is full of myths, and blackjack is no exception. If you're going to become a serious blackjack player with any real chance of success, you're going to have to get over the irrational instincts that plague so many gamblers. Following are a half dozen prevalent myths that you're probably going to have to *un-learn* at the blackjack tables.

Blackjack Myth #1

"Figure the Dealer for a
10 in the hole"

Here's a prevalent piece of common "street knowledge" about blackjack that belongs right in the toilet. When learning the game, players are often advised to play their hands as though the dealer's hole card is a *10*. This silly credo tends to stick with many of them for the rest of their lives. For example, many players will look at this hand;

and call it "*12* against a *12*". *That gets you into trouble, right there!* Why? It's true that there are four times as many *10's* in a blackjack deck as any other card. But there are still 2$\frac{1}{4}$ times as many *non-10's* as *10's*! The fact is, since only about 30% of all the cards are *10's*;

THE DEALER WILL HAVE SOME OTHER
CARD IN THE HOLE 70% OF THE TIME

Get this straight. A dealer's *deuce* up is not *12* -- *it's 2!* In fact, when the dealer has a *deuce* up, she's actually more likely to have a pretty good drawing hand than *12*. These five cards;

will all give her *7* through *11*, where only four cards will stick her with *12* specifically.

Assuming that the dealer has a *10* in the hole would be exactly the same as assuming that the next card out of the shoe is a *10*, or that any face-down card anywhere is a *10*. If that was true, where the heck would all those *10's* come from when 216 cards out of a 312 card shoe are some other kind of card?

The "*10* in the hole" assumption is much too vague a guideline for accurate hand play, and will lead to costly mistakes down the road. Think about it. If the dealer's really supposed to have a *10* in the hole, you'd split your pair of *10's* against a *5* up. You'd also double down with *7* against a dealer's *6* because what the heck -- she's got *16!* And you'd probably have to hit with *10/7* against a *face-card* because after all, *17* doesn't beat *20*. The list of silly errors goes on and on.

The correct play for any hand as always, is based upon all the different cards the dealer can have in the hole, how often she'll have each of them, which cards she can catch if she must hit again, and how often you'll catch each of the different cards available to you. Only after weighing each of these factors accurately can you proceed efficiently with the play of your hand. But don't bother to get out your slide rule yet, because the basic strategy has already done all that legwork for you.

Just remember this. Every time the dealer has an *Ace* up, the house will lay you 2-to-1 odds that the *10* isn't underneath it *(the Insurance option). Why do you suppose they're doing that??* So just lose that "dealer's *10* in the hole" mentality and play your hands according to the correct basic strategy from the get-go!

30

Blackjack Myth #2

"I'm Due to Win"

Please -- stop guessing whether you'll win your next bet based upon what's been happening up to now. If it had anything to do with that, there'd be winners all over the place. Yet, most gamblers do believe that the recent past does influence the immediate future. It's a widespread instinctive belief that generates from a basic, but almost universal misunderstanding of how chance events work.

How many times have you seen a blackjack player sit down and begin to play very poised at first? Then after losing four or five hands in a row, he raises his bet from $15 up to $50 or $75 on the next hand. Why? Because he was, "due to win", of course! After all, this person knows he has to win a bet sooner or later -- so that winning hand must be growing more and more likely with each deal, right? *Wrong!*

Remember, that big blackjack accountant in the sky *(mentioned in Chapter One)* only exists in your mind. The gambling gods couldn't care less about evening out the score, and the law of averages couldn't care less either. The cards don't know you've just lost five in a row, and you're not any more likely to win your next hand because of it*. Sure, things will come close to balancing out eventually because the odds are so close to 50-50. That's a given. But *eventually* is the key word here.

Hey, wait a minute! Notice that on one hand I'm pro-claiming you're never "due" to win -- yet on the other hand I'm conceding that things will eventually even out. Well, how can these two things both be true at the same time? *Now, listen carefully; this is important.*

---

*Technically in blackjack, the player tends to do better with high cards, and the dealer wins more often with low cards. So if the player has lost several consecutive hands, there is a slightly elevated probability that he has used up an abundance of small cards in doing so. Hence, there could be a surplus of undealt high cards at this point in the deal. But this is an unrelated and negligible factor, applicable to blackjack alone. To consider it here would only be misleading.

If you decided to flip a coin 100 times, you'd be right to expect 50 heads and 50 tails. But what if the first 20 tosses happened to come up all heads? How many heads should you have at the end of your 100 flips *now?* If you brought in a professional Las Vegas oddsmaker to set an *"over/under"* betting line on this, what should his number be? Should it still be 50 total heads? No -- the answer is **60.** Why? Because no matter what's happened thus far;

THE REMAINING 80 TOSSES SHOULD STILL PRODUCE 40 HEADS, ON AVERAGE!

That's what'll happen more often than anything else. *"But wouldn't that be a total of 60% heads instead of 50%?"*, you ask. Yes it would be. That's because those 10 extra heads *(in the first 20 tosses)* weren't likely to come up, *but they did*. Still, the most likely thing to happen from here on out is *always* the most normal thing! There is absolutely *no* tendency for tails to come up next.

But then, how do things balance out in the long run? *Stay with me -- we're almost home.* Let's say that because of such a wacky start, you decided to extend this little flipping experiment out to one million tosses, including the 20 flips you've just finished. How many total heads are you most likely to have when you're done? Remember -- all the remaining tosses should produce half heads and half tails. Then you'd have 500,010 heads, total -- still the same 10 heads above 50%. But the overall percentage of heads would fall to **50.001%**! That's what's meant by, *"Lop-sided results are not corrected; they just fade into the past."*

Do you see what's happened here? The ever-accumulating number of *normal* outcomes has diluted the impact of those first 20 straight heads until they've become virtually meaningless.

THAT'S THE ONLY KIND OF "EVENING OUT" PROCESS THAT ACTUALLY OCCURS

You might have been losing profusely, but rest assured, the gambling gods don't give a rat's ass! If the remaining cards give you a 49% chance to win the next hand -- then that's your chance of winning it no matter how many in a row you may have won or lost up to now. This, you must learn to believe, *or you've already lost!* You're never "due" to win!

32

Blackjack Myth #3

"You can Beat the House by Quitting when You're Ahead"

You see it all the time. Blackjack players come up to the table, buy in for maybe 10 bets, try to get a little ahead, and then scram. When a player like this gets out in front, you can see it on his face. He glances at his chips, then looks at his watch. He has one eye on the cards and one eye on the door.

What these players are trying to do is make money at blackjack by quitting when they're ahead. It would seem to make sense. I mean if you always quit while you're a winner, that has to give you an edge -- *doesn't it?*

Well, no it doesn't! Let me explain why. What do you suppose your chances are of beating an honest deck cutting game? All you have to do is guess "red" or "black" and cut the deck. Then shuffle, guess and cut again. The answer of course is -- you're a 50-50 shot. But did you know there's a way to book a winner on roughly 80% of your playing sessions in this game if you manage your money right? How? *Simply by quitting every time you get one bet ahead.*

The only losers you'll ever book are when you lose your first cut and never get ahead, even for a moment. As good as 80% sounds though, it's *not* a winning strategy. There's still one problem you can't get away from. No matter what, *you're going to end up winning 50% of all your cuts.* And at even money per cut, where does that put you? *Dead even* — doesn't it?

Let's look at this principle from a blackjack standpoint. What if you were a good enough blackjack player that you've broken dead even over the past ten years? So to gain a little extra edge, you decide you're going to quit any time your winnings should dwindle to a pre-determined minimum?

Now let's say that on two consecutive days you quickly found yourself winning $500, then slipped to being only $200 ahead. True to your game plan, you locked up the $200 win both

33

times and high-tailed it home. For those two sessions then, your blackjack log would look like this;

WIN	+$200
WIN	+$200
	+$400

That's two wins, no losses and a $400 gain. By quitting winners, you've averted the possibility of any losses and can start out fresh next time as another 50-50 shot.   But you've also averted something else -- and that's the possibility of a larger win. You see, as a break even player, you would've been as likely to win a few more dollars as lose back that same amount had you kept on playing. In fact if you played onward both times, climbing upward another $500 once, and dropping down $500 the other time would be perfectly *normal* and *average* for a break even player, wouldn't it? Then your blackjack log would look like this;

WIN	+$700
LOSE	-$300
	+$400

Now you'd have one win and one loss, but the same $400 net gain. *Stop right here and think hard about that.* Since you're just as likely to win as lose overall, both events will occur equally often if you always choose to keep playing. But it'll all net you the same total result as quitting to lock up a winner. This is a prime example of the fact that:

YOU CAN'T IMPROVE YOUR CHANCES OF WINNING OVERALL JUST BY STARTING AND STOPPING AT SELECTIVE POINTS

Quitting a winner will only work if you never gamble again. But if you're just going to come back and play another time, then there's no difference between the hand you missed because you quit -- and the first hand of your next session!

Quitting and starting over may have given your *mind* a sense of closure, but to the cards and the chips, *it's all just the next hand.* That's because gambling is really all one long game even if we don't think of it that way. No matter how many times you may start and stop along the way, you're still going down that same road to *Losersville* if you can't play a winning class of game.

Gamblers tend to measure their successes and failures by the day, as if it were a baseball or football game. But our pocketbooks can't feel where one day ended and the next began. When you quit just to lock up a guaranteed winner, you're merely stopping to admire your progress at a favorable interval. That interrupts, but doesn't alter your progress. You might as well sit at the table and say to yourself, *"Okay, I'm $200 ahead; I quit".* Then get out a notebook, log down your $200 winner and take the next hand.

IT'S THE SAME AS LEAVING
AND COMING BACK NEXT WEEK

By now you may be thinking to yourself, *"What's he telling me, don't gamble?"* No, I'm not! What I am saying is, don't be deluded into believing you can win with irrelevant tactics.

Just understand that if you're basically a losing player, you're always more likely to lose than win whether it's right now or tomorrow. There's simply no other day on the calendar where you can escape that. The only way to become a sustained winner at any form of gambling is to be betting the long end of the stick. That means having a legitimate outright advantage. I'm sorry, but;

TRYING TO TIME YOUR LUCK JUST WON'T WORK

The more you focus on irrelevant game tactics such as these, the less aware you'll be of things that really do matter. Then you'll just be another frustrated loser, and won't even realize why.

Blackjack Myth #4

"The Order of the Cards is Sacred"

Remember when you were a kid, playing poker on your kitchen table for pennies and nickels? How did you feel when the dealer made a mistake, and you wound up receiving something other than your correct cards? If you're anything like I was as a youngster, you probably felt jinxed.

Well, old beliefs die hard. Very often in the casino when a new player steps up to the blackjack table in the middle of a shoe, somebody asks him if he would mind waiting until the shuffle. This person's curious request usually stems from the same old fear that the new player is going to corrupt the *"sacred"* order of three or four hundred randomly shuffled cards -- *and that it's destined to work against the players.*

Can you honestly explain where this fear comes from? If blindly changing the order of the cards can work against the player, couldn't it possibly work against the dealer too? Let me ask you this question;

IF YOU COULD HAND PICK YOUR CARDS, FACE-DOWN FROM ANYWHERE IN THE SHOE, WHICH ONES WOULD YOU TAKE?

Stumped? Then how could you prefer one face-down card over another? And why in the world should the card you would have gotten be *good* for you, but *bad* for the player who actually ends up getting it because of the extra hand that was dealt? You get the same static from other players when somebody at the table decides to start playing two hands instead of one, or one instead of two. In all these cases, the order of the cards has been changed. *But will it change them for the better, or for the worse??*

When I play blackjack, even if I knew exactly which cards were left in the shoe, I still wouldn't know their order. So I would never know whether I preferred my own card, or the card of the player next to me. When I double down, it's because based on the *overall* odds, taking exactly one more blind card from *all* those that remain is likely to make me a winning hand. But I don't know whether the very next card is any more likely to do it for me than the one after it. In fact, *I really wouldn't care if the cocktail waitress leaned over and pulled it out from the middle of the shoe!* I left that superstition at the kitchen table when I was a kid.

Most serious blackjack players object to the order of the cards being changed only when things are going well. And if they're losing, then they in fact *want* to change the cards around so as to break the dealer's "hot streak". This suggests that if you're winning, then the *following* cards in the shoe are stacked in your favor, and shouldn't be tampered with. But in reality, all it means is that the *previous* cards in the shoe *were* stacked in your favor.

An enlightening study on just this kind of "streakiness" was reported on in Stanford Wong's highly recommended book, *Professional Blackjack.* In that experiment, 20 million computer hands were run, recording the win/lose results for the player immediately following two consecutive wins, two consecutive losses, and every other possible two hand combination of wins, losses and ties. The results?

VIRTUALLY NO DIFFERENCE BETWEEN ANY OF THEM!

The player was no more likely to win his next hand just after having won two in a row, than immediately after losing two in a row. So then, what is there to be preserved in the order of the cards? In that regard, every next hand is a brand new ball game.

More and more in casinos today, signs are showing up on the blackjack tables that read, **"No Mid-shoe Entry"**. That means a new player may enter the game only at the beginning of each new shoe. These signs are more common at the higher stakes tables. Superstitious gamblers say it was done to stop new players from jinxing the incumbents at the table by changing the order of the cards. Now, it *is* possible that casino management may have decided to pacify some of their more superstitious high rollers with this accommodation. But rest assured, there's at least one much more important reason why those signs are there. That's to stop card counters from standing back while counting down a shoe, and then stepping up and making large bets when the deck composition turns favorable for the players. Mind you, deck composition is an entirely different thing than "the order of the cards".

You see, when a card counter does this, it's not because he knows he wants the very next card out of the shoe. He only knows that the remaining cards, *in their entirety* now contain lots of *10's* and *Aces.* And that's better for the player than it is for the dealer. At these times;

HE'D BE JUST AS HAPPY TO BE DEALT TWO CARDS FROM THE BACK OF THE SHOE AS FROM THE FRONT

So then, why should *you* worry about it? As it all turns out, the casino has the best of both worlds in their **"No Mid-shoe Entry"** games. They thwart card counters and appease superstitious blackjack players at the same time.

As for you, don't let the presence of a new player at the table throw you off your game. You have enough to think about without being distracted over things that will only wash out over time. Just play whatever cards you do get the right way, and stay focused on things that you know can make a positive difference.

Blackjack Myth #5

"Bad Players at the Table Hurt You"

It's a dreaded phobia that festers in the hearts of most blackjack players; the fear that the stranger at third base will misplay his hand, causing you to lose in the process. This belief that bad players hurt a good player's chances is so widespread that many die-hard *"21"* buffs refuse to play in the company of novices! What does it all amount to in the big picture? *Jack Squat -- that's what!* Furthermore, I believe I can prove it to you if you'll just follow along with me.

Suppose you were playing blackjack with only one other person at the table. You're at first base and he's at third. The dealer has a *deuce* up. You're both dealt a *15*. Acting first, you make the correct play and stand. Now it's the third baseman's turn. You realize the dealer has to bust -- or you lose. *So how do you want third base to play his hand?*

If you said, *"Stand"*, can you in logical terms explain why? Are you afraid that if he makes a mistake and hits it'll be bad luck for you? This is a common paranoia with no logical basis. But where does this paranoia come from? It stems from the fear of what can happen amidst threatening uncertainty.

First, there's the threatening uncertainty of what the dealer has in the hole. Then there's the threatening uncertainty of what the next card out of the shoe will be --- *or the one after it*. Put that all together and most people wish the third baseman would just "play it by the book", and stand. Does that sound like you?

Well then, the picture on the following page will supply some answers to all this uncertainty. Notice when you look at it that we were slick enough to get a peek the dealer's hole card. Gosh darn if it isn't a *face-card*, giving her *12*. But that's not all. Hell, I've just bribed the dealer into flashing us a glimpse of the next two cards in the shoe! Go ahead, have a look at them.

39

THE NEXT 2 CARDS

As you can see, they're a *9* and a *10,* but she flashed them so quickly that we couldn't tell which card was first and which was second. So there; now you know everything there is to know except for the final outcome.

Now I have to ask you again. *How do you want the third baseman to play his hand?* Notice that if he hits, no matter which card comes first, he loses. And if he stands, he's got a 50-50 shot at winning. So obviously, hitting is the wrong play *for him.* But how does that affect *your* chances? Let's see.

If the third baseman *stands* like you probably want him to, and the *9* is first out of the shoe, the dealer makes *21.* But if the *10* comes first, the dealer busts.

Now instead, what happens if the third baseman *hits*? Well, when the *9* comes first, the dealer gets the *10* and busts. But if the *10* is first, the dealer makes *21* with the *9!* Now, I'm going to ask you one last time. *How do you want the third baseman to play his hand?*

40

Can you see that while hitting his hand is a horrible play for Mr. 3rd Base, *your odds to win remain the same no matter what he does?* That's absolutely true because your chance to win does not depend upon how third base plays his hand;

BUT UPON WHICH CARD COMES NEXT OUT OF THE SHOE!

Many times it won't matter whether the dealer gets the first or second card -- they'll either both make him or break him. But when it does matter, you never know which is going to be which! *So, being all concerned over whether third base stands or hits is just plain silly!*

Now, your immediate response to this may be that it only works this way because of the particular hypothetical situation that I've set up manually. Well then, go ahead and replace the dealer's hole card with any other you wish. Also replace the next two cards in the shoe with any others as well. You'll find that it'll always come down to that same question of whether the first or second card out of the shoe is better for the dealer.

PUTTIN' IT TO THE TEST: I know that many of you

reading this right now just aren't buying it. But what if I produced a little something physical you could grab onto? In my home with my own six deck shoe, I dealt 500 rounds of blackjack with me sitting at first base and the mythical "Player from Hell" at third. I played all 500 of my hands according to perfect basic strategy while third base misplayed every one of his hands -- *bar none!* If he was dealt *16* against a *5*, he hit it. If he had *7* against a *face-card,* he stood pat. He always split a pair of *5's* or *10's* and doubled down with blackjack. Now there's a bad player for you!

After each round was complete, I wrote down a "W", an "L" or a "P" for the result of my hand only *(I ignored third base's results completely).* Then I reviewed the cards to see how I'd have made out had third base played his hand correctly, and wrote my "woulda' been" result in an adjacent column.

How did all that come out? First, it's interesting to note that third base's 500 consecutive mistakes changed my own outcome on only 95 hands. The other 405 times, it wouldn't have mattered.

But what happened on those 95 pivotal hands? I'd like to be able to tell you that it all went 50-50, but then 500 hands isn't a lifetime of blackjack either. Here are the actual raw scores:

	w/ 3rd Base playing correctly	w/ 3rd Base misplaying every hand
I won:	257$\frac{1}{2}$	263$\frac{1}{2}$
I lost:	266	264
I pushed:	40	36

Both totals add up to more than 500 due to doubles, splits and blackjacks. Now, gambling being what it is, things won't come out exactly this way every time. Either way though, there's absolutely nothing in these 500 hands to even hint that 3rd Base's *horrendous* play might have a tendency to hurt somebody else's results.

THE CLINCHER: This raging debate has been argued every which way but one – *mathematically.* Shouldn't there be a way to mathematically *prove* whether somebody's bad play hurts another player's chances? Well, there is! What's more, it's a simple proof that can be expressed in logical, layman's terms.

Look back at the picture on page 40. But this time, the last *four* cards left before the cut card will be *three 10s* and still *one 9,* again in unknown order. Now we'll count how many times out of four the dealer will break if 3rd Base *stands* – then compare that to how many times out of four the dealer will break if 3rd Base *hits*.

If 3rd Base Stands:
:**Dealer pulls a *10* and breaks -- *three* times out of *four*.**

If 3rd Base Hits:
:3rd Base takes a *10* – *three* times out of *four*.
:dealer then pulls a *10* and *breaks* – *two* of those *three* times.
:3rd Base takes the *9* one time out of *four*. That *one* time in *four,* the dealer must *break* with one of the three remaining *10s*.
:**Dealer breaks *three* times out of *four* if 3rd Base hits.**

Most players are paranoid about 3rd Base hitting, since if he takes a *10,* it improves the dealer's chances to make a hand. But 3rd Base can also take a small card – which improves the dealer's chances to bust. The thing of it is – *the effects of these two probabilities will always cancel each other out* – with *any* card composition!

Blackjack Myth #6

"Progressive Betting Systems can Overcome the House Edge"

This sixth and final topic of the chapter must be presented as an "assumed" myth, since its validity has never been disproved beyond the shadow of a doubt. So read the evidence carefully and reach your conclusion responsibly.

Every day, hoards of gamblers storm the casinos armed with some form of betting progression. With progressive betting, you size every next bet according to the previous outcome. Each progressionist feels that his particular betting system should **win** more money than it **loses**, even though it will **lose** more bets than it **wins**. What a neat trick! Can it work? Well, if you're analyzing it from a *purely mathematical* standpoint, it cannot! Here's why.

First, let's clarify that there are *positive* progressions and *negative* progressions -- but most progressive betting systems are the *positive* type. That is, you increase your bet after a win, and reduce it after a loss. This is supposed to show a net profit after everything shakes out by taking advantage of your winning streaks. As a working example, let's take a look at a popular progressive betting system known as the "1-2-3-5 step-up" progression. Here's how that works:

You start out betting 1 unit and stick to a 1 unit bet if you lose. But if you win, you progress to a 2 unit wager and if you win again, increase it to 3 units. If you win your third consecutive bet, you progress to a 5 unit wager and stay there as long as you keep winning. But you will always revert to a 1 unit wager immediately following any loss on any step of the progression.

Now suppose you were gambling with your buddy on a totally even proposition such as the flip of a coin. If you were just flat betting *(same size bet on every flip)* you'd stand to break even over the long haul since you should win as many flips as you lose. But how would you make out if you used the 1-2-3-5 betting progression?

Well, on the surface the system looks like a winner because if you win four bets in a row you gain 11 units *(1+2+3+5)* -- but if you lose four straight it costs you only four units *(1+1+1+1)*. So far, so good! Now what happens if you win three and lose one, or win one and lose three? How about when you go two and two? For all those answers, let's look at the chart below:

WWWW	**+11**	**WWLL**	**-1**	**WLLL**	**-3**
WWWL	**+1**	**WLWL**	**-2**	**LWLL**	**-3**
WWLW	**+1**	**WLLW**	**-1**	**LLWL**	**-3**
WLWW	**+2**	**LWWL**	**-1**	**LLLW**	**-2**
LWWW	**+5**	**LWLW**	**-1**	**LLLL**	**-4**
		LLWW	**+1**		

This takes in every possible outcome for when you make four bets. Nothing has been left out. As you can see, your results for a particular sequence of outcomes depends not only upon how many wins and losses you have, but also on the order they come in. Of course, your biggest swings occur when your results come in a "streaky" formation. You must however, take all sequences into consideration since they'll all eventually occur. Just noting your results when "this" or "that" happens will mislead you. But now I have to ask you a very important question:

WHICH OF THOSE 16 OUTCOMES
IS MOST LIKELY TO OCCUR?

Think about it. The answer is, *they are all equally likely!* That's right! *"WWWW"* is exactly as likely as *"LLLL"* or even *"WLWL specifically"* for that matter. Oh, it's true that it's much easier to go 2 and 2 than it is to go 4 and 0 -- or 0 and 4. But there's only one way to win them all or lose them all, and there are *six* ways to go 2 and 2 *(the entire center row)!* The thing of it is, any single *W* is just as likely as any *L,* and that makes any **specific sequence** of outcomes just as likely as any other! Got that? If not, go back and read these last two paragraphs again.

Alrighty then, notice that the result each sequence would produce is shown to its right. *Now here comes the interesting part.* Add up all the sequences that produce a gain and you get 21 units won. Now go ahead and add up all the sequences that produce a loss and what do you get? You get 21 units lost.

Time to stop and think again. Now we know that all 16 sequences are equally likely to occur. Some of them produce a loss while the others yield a gain. But since they're all equally likely, where would we be if we bet on four flips of a coin 16 different times and got every different sequence once each? We'd be dead even, wouldn't we? Well, *over the fullness of time, that's just what we'll get!*

So when you bet on four flips of a coin using this betting progression, it's like drawing a slip of paper out of a hat that contains 16 slips of paper in all -- each one with a different four flip sequence written on it? Since all the pluses add up to the same number as all the minuses, *you're still a 50-50 shot in a 50-50 game!*

The only unbalanced part is that you have a chance to score a bigger winner than your maximum loser --- but there are more losing slips of paper in the hat! These two inequalities offset each other perfectly. The way it works out is that;

BETTING PROGRESSIONS GATHER THE BULK OF YOUR WINS INTO A CONDENSED AREA -- YOUR STREAKS.

Then they spread out your smaller losses across a broader range *(notice that going 2 and 2 usually costs you money)*. But your overall edge *(or disadvantage)* remains unchanged!

Now -- this is not some "black magic" that occurs with the 1-2-3-5 progression alone. On the contrary, *the exact same thing is true of any progression --- positive, negative or regressive!* Sound too hokey to be true? Go ahead, try out your own home spun concoction on the win/lose chart right now! You'll always find that the total units won and total units lost add up to the same number. *Fascinated???*

Well guess what? There's still more! It also doesn't matter whether you play your progression for 4 bets, 40 bets or 4000 bets! That's because for *any* number of bets there are just *exactly* so many possible win/lose sequences that they can come in.

45

You see, with 4 bets there are just 16 ways things can come out -- which makes it easy to see what's going on. With 10 bets there are 1024 ways -- no more, no less. And with 100 bets the answer is a big honkin' 31 digit number! But it really doesn't matter, because if you laid them all out on paper and added together the gains from all the winning sequences, they will always equal the total losses sustained by all the losing sequences. And when you gamble, you'll just be drawing one of those sequences out of that big hat *whose slips of paper all add up to zero!* That's no edge!

So with progressions, winning streaks win big and losing streaks lose more moderately. But *here's the part that few people realize* -- if your sequence contains exactly as many wins as losses;

YOU'LL MOSTLY LIKELY LOSE A LITTLE, RATHER THAN BREAK EVEN

That's because going WLWLWL, etc. costs you money with a positive betting progression. After you add your *moderate* losses from your losing streaks together with your *minimal* losses accumulated through the prolonged chops, they will exactly equal the *larger* amount won during your winning streaks -- once all phases have occurred. Your progression has merely *redistributed* the gains and losses without changing the bottom line. So what does it all mean? It means that.........

MATHEMATICALLY SPEAKING, BETTING PROGRESSIONS CANNOT GIVE YOU AN EDGE!

But you must understand. Progressive betting systems are not *losing* systems. Indeed they are *"break even"* systems. When betting progressions lose in casino games such as roulette or craps, it's not because they are losing systems. It's because they are *break even* systems used in a *losing* game.

The Card-Clumping Debate: So now we see that betting progressions can't work in an *unbiased process* because once all sequences occur as often as they're supposed to, you're right back where you started. A huge controversy enters the picture however,

when betting progressions are applied to the game of blackjack. It all stems from the following question.

"What if there was something preventing all sequences from occurring as often as they're supposed to in blackjack?" Just suppose all those mundane combinations of 2 wins and 2 losses from the center column in the win/lose chart somehow occurred *less* -- and the streaks occurred *more*. If that were true, then there would be more +11's and -4's -- but fewer +1's and -2's. Then betting progressions could in fact produce a net gain!

Many blackjack players believe *card clumping* causes just that very thing to occur in blackjack. Gamblers have been saying for 25 years that shoe games seem to run more streaky than hand held decks. For that reason, some blackjack players insist their own personal betting progressions are a winning formula.

What about it? Do streaks really occur more often in multi-deck blackjack than the odds say. Lengthy computer simulations say they *don't*. But most computers shuffle the cards perfectly, forcing them into random order. Proponents of progressive betting cite *imperfect* human shuffles as the culprit of streakiness. They say the players' drawing and standing strategies tend to leave high cards clumped with high cards, and lows with lows. This they maintain is not obliterated by a manual shuffle, causing players to win more consecutive hands through high card clumps, then lose more successive hands through low card clumps.

To prove *conclusively* that this doesn't happen in the *material* world would require a mammoth hand dealt experiment. That I don't have. The best I can do is offer a little something empirical to toss back and forth concerning this hotly debated topic.

I own a copy of Bob Hubby's book, the *Blackjack Tracker*. Bob Hubby used to be a casino blackjack dealer. Using a physical six deck shoe and a standard casino shuffle, he dealt 13,000 rounds of blackjack to four player positions -- 52,000 hands in all. Then he recorded every win loss and tie in order -- and published the entire tabulation as a book. Starting at the beginning of that book, I cataloged every streak of exactly 3 wins in a row that occurred through the first 10,000 rounds in seat #1.

47

Now the straight mathematical probabilities for winning, losing and pushing a hand of multi-deck blackjack are $43^1/2$%, 48% and $8^1/2$% respectively. Based upon that, you'd expect to win exactly 3 consecutive hands 263 times over the course of 10,000 hands dealt. The actual tally from *Blackjack Tracker* is listed below:

	THE ODDS SAY	ACTUAL RESULTS
3 (exactly) STRAIGHT WINS IN **10,000** DEALT HANDS	**263**	**267**

Admittedly, this was quite a limited sample size. In 10,000 *other* hands, you might get --- *well-l-l* --- just how many "3 in a rows" *could* you get in 10,000 other hands? Based upon this finding, there's but 1 statistical chance in 50 that the next 10,000 hands would produce as many as 300 such streaks.

So what have we got? On one hand we have a mere 10,000 blackjack hands which produced a number of winning streaks that fell very close to their *random* probability. And on the other hand we have lots of gamblers who recollect that their shoes seem to run awfully streaky. But did they *keep track* of how many streaks they actually had? Did they even know how many streaks they were *supposed* to have in the first place? How many extra streaks would it take before they could casually notice that it must not be random? Sounds like another case of selective memory perception. When you have a nice streak, you remember it. The chops? *What's to remember?* Here's what we know for sure about progressive betting systems:

A) If streaks occur merely as often as they're supposed to in multi-deck play, there's no way betting progressions can alter the player's expectation. Blackjack would then be hopelessly locked into the same mathematical constraints with craps, roulette and a coin flip.
B) Most typical players instinctively uses some sort of progressive approach to their betting, and almost none of them are winners.

Until somebody puts together a few hundred thousand manually dealt blackjack hands and records the occurrence of streaks within, we'll have to go with what we know. Based upon that, it's all but certain that blackjack *cannot* be beaten with a betting progression.

Chapter 4
KEY POINTS

1) Gambling tends to attract individuals who believe it possesses mystical qualities and secret keys to easy success. It doesn't.

2) Blackjack players are bred to assume that the dealer has a *10* in the hole. In reality, she will have some other card 70% of the time.

3) The average gambler feels that a string of unusual events is predisposed to swing back in the opposite direction, so as to even things out. It's not!

4) Most gamblers think you can improve your overall cumulative results by quitting at choice intervals, and starting up again at a later date. You can't!

5) Many typical blackjack players feel that the order of the cards is "sacred" and shouldn't be tampered with. It doesn't matter!

6) Most blackjack players can't let go of the notion that it's "unlucky" to play with bad players. It's not!

7) The majority of blackjack players are convinced that following some sort of "betting" system will improve their overall results. This is highly unlikely!

SECTION C

Proper Blackjack Strategy

5
the *Basic Strategy*

In the game of casino blackjack you can be dealt 340 different basic hand situations. When you have *13* and the dealer shows a *6*, that's a hand situation. *16* against a *10* up is another.

About a hundred of these hand situations play themselves. By that I mean, nobody with two brain cells to rub together needs to be told how to play them -- they're automatic. Some of these no-brainers are when you've been dealt a total of *5* against the dealer's *face-card*, or a *19* against a *4* up. A *genius* and a *moron* would both play these hands the same way.

The other two hundred and some odd hands however are more debatable. How about when you have a pair of *6's* and the dealer shows a *3?* Should you split the *6's* - take a hit - or just stand with *12?* Questions like these should not be answered intuitively, because they're really a matter of mathematics. Unlike some card games such as poker, casino blackjack playing strategy is entirely devoid of psychology.

Every day, thousands upon thousands of gamblers throw their money away at the blackjack tables when they "wing" it by trying to infuse their own personalized logic into the play of their hands. And it's so unnecessary, because all the right plays have already been determined.

THE "BASIC STRATEGY" IS THE MATHEMATICALLY
MOST ADVANTAGEOUS WAY TO PLAY EACH HAND
(without regard for the cards that have already been eliminated)

It has been calculated, simulated, refined and re-refined with computers since the late 1950's. Modern basic strategy was developed by first removing the 3 combined cards that make up the player's starting hand and the dealer's up-card from the "imaginary" deck. Then, every combination of cards that can be drawn for each way to play that hand was calculated and evaluated, indicating the most efficient play. Later, billions of computer simulated hands were run, verifying and refining the accuracy of those earlier calculations. Out of all that was born the correct basic strategy of play. With it, the casino's edge over you in a typical multi-deck blackjack game would be just about $^1/2\%$. With fewer decks, it would be smaller yet. In a few rare single deck games, a perfect basic strategy player has no disadvantage at all. *(See "Rule Variations" at the end of this chapter)*.

Without the basic strategy, blackjack would just be another casino table game that has the player hopelessly outgunned. But fortunately, "21" is complex enough that most players make plenty of mistakes with their hands, and that's where the bulk of the casino's profit comes from. This is what enables the house to continue offering a game in which they'd have almost no edge if you played all your hands correctly.

For a stark "newbie" at blackjack however, playing every single hand correctly can be a pretty tall order. Memorizing a complex looking chart full of 270 multi-colored squares can become bewildering. For them a few sound basics might be fine; the small details can come later.

If that sounds like you, there *is* something simpler than jumping right into the complete basic strategy. It's called *"The Blackjack Starter Kit"*. It condenses the entire basic strategy down to just seven fundamental rules. Mind you however that;

...THESE ARE NOT PERFECT, NOR TOTALLY COMPLETE!

Most of the trickier plays have been ignored in the interest of simplicity. But by using these fundamentals, you'll still be playing most of your hands accurately and you'll be approaching the game along the right lines. When the time comes that you want more complete information, your transition to the full, correct basic strategy should be relatively smooth.

BLACKJACK STARTER KIT

1) **Stop** *at 12 if the dealer shows a 6 or lower.*
2) **Hit** *until 17 or bust if the dealer shows a 7 or higher.*
3) **Hit** *w/ Ace/6 or lower &* **Stand** *w/ Ace/7 or higher.*
4) **Double Down** *w/ 10 or 11 whenever you've got the dealer beaten on board.*
5) *Always* **Split** *a pair of Aces or 8s – no matter what!*
6) **Split** *a pair of 7s if the dealer shows a 7 or lower.*
7) *Never take* **Insurance** *or* **Even Money**.

That's it! To clarify, hit *any soft 17* or lower, but stand with a *soft 18* or higher. Double down if your two-card *10* or *11* is higher than the dealer's up-card *(such as with 6/4 against her 9 or with 8/3 against a 10)*. Split no other pairs than *Aces*, *8s* and *7s* as noted, and simply forget the Insurance rule even exists.

    If you can just get these seven starter rules tucked under your belt, the casino's edge will have been trimmed down to just about 1% in a typical multi-deck game. That means playing **100** hands and finishing **one** bet behind if you have perfectly *normal* luck. Picking up that last available ½% using perfect basic strategy will involve splitting some extra scattered pairs, adding some hard and soft double downs and correcting a few hard and soft hits. When you're ready to fine-tune those, it's time to digest a complete basic strategy chart, which follows.

ON TO THE BASIC STRATEGY

Basic strategies have been developed for single deck, double deck, 4 deck, 6 deck and 8 deck games with various rules for each. Although there's not much difference between any two strategies, knowing the right one for the rules and number of decks you're playing with can be worth up to a few hundredths percent. The color-coded master chart on the next page is right for 4-to-8 decks

53

when the dealer **stands** on *soft 17.* You can double down on any first two cards, but **not** after splits, and you can re-split pairs out to four hands, except for *Aces* which receive only one card each.

The BASIC STRATEGY

HIT	STAND	
DOUBLE	SPLIT	

4 to 8 decks /stand on soft 17 /No double after split

DEALER'S UP-CARD

YOU	2	3	4	5	6	7	8	9	10	A
8	H	H	H	H	H	H	H	H	H	H
9	H	D	D	D	D	H	H	H	H	H
10	D	D	D	D	D	D	D	D	H	H
11	D	D	D	D	D	D	D	D	D	H
12	H	H	S	S	S	H	H	H	H	H
13	S	S	S	S	S	H	H	H	H	H
14	S	S	S	S	S	H	H	H	H	H
15	S	S	S	S	S	H	H	H	H	H
16	S	S	S	S	S	H	H	H	H	H
17	S	S	S	S	S	S	S	S	S	S
A/2	H	H	H	D	D	H	H	H	H	H
A/3	H	H	H	D	D	H	H	H	H	H
A/4	H	H	D	D	D	H	H	H	H	H
A/5	H	H	D	D	D	H	H	H	H	H
A/6	H	D	D	D	D	H	H	H	H	H
A/7	S	D	D	D	D	S	S	H	H	H
A/8	S	S	S	S	S	S	S	S	S	S
2/2	H	H	SP	SP	SP	SP	H	H	H	H
3/3	H	H	SP	SP	SP	SP	H	H	H	H
4/4	H	H	H	H	H	H	H	H	H	H
5/5	D	D	D	D	D	D	D	D	H	H
6/6	H	SP	SP	SP	SP	H	H	H	H	H
7/7	SP	SP	SP	SP	SP	SP	H	H	H	H
8/8	SP	SP	SP	SP	SP	SP	SP	SP	SP	SP
9/9	SP	SP	SP	SP	SP	S	SP	SP	S	S
10/10	S	S	S	S	S	S	S	S	S	S
A/A	SP	SP	SP	SP	SP	SP	SP	SP	SP	SP

Although there are 340 hands you can be dealt, the chart contains only 270 squares. That's because certain things are assumed to be foregone conclusions. For example, if you'll never double down with a total of *8*, then it's a forgone conclusion that you'll never double down with *less* than *8*. Hence, totals of *7* or less are not on the chart. Also, since you'll always stand with any hard *17*, then you'll always stand with *more* than a hard *17*.

The next few charts are addendum to the color chart. They tell you what to do when you're playing with different rules or numbers of decks. Many casinos for example, allow you to double down on new hands that were created by splitting a pair. A classic example would be when you split two *7's* and catch a *4* on your first *7*, then double down with your new *11*. If the house you're in allows "double after split" *(DAS)*, then there are seven additional pairs that it becomes advantageous for you to split. The following chart defines those hands with an **"spl"** in the box.

Basic Strategy
When *"DOUBLE AFTER SPLIT"* is allowed

DEALER'S UP-CARD

HAND	2	3	4	5	6
2/2	spl	spl			
3/3	spl	spl			
4/4				spl	spl
6/6	spl				

In some games the dealer must hit a *soft 17*. Even though this tends to improve her hand, she'll sometimes bust her *soft 17* when she hits it. Hence, you should double down with these two hands.

Basic Strategy
When Dealer *HITS SOFT 17*

DEALER'S UP-CARD

HAND	2	3	4	5	6	7	8	9	10	A
11										dbl
A/8					dbl					

55

In a few casinos, blackjack is dealt with one or two decks. Following are the hands that should be played differently in *double* deck *21*. **"dbl"** stands for "double; **"spl"** means to "split" the pair.

Basic Strategy
DOUBLE DECK blackjack

DEALER'S UP-CARD

HAND	2	3	4	5	6	7	8	9	10	A
9	dbl									
11										dbl
A/3			dbl							
6/6	spl									

In *single* deck *21*, every exposed card affects the remaining ones more, since there are so few of them. A prime example is a pair of *7's* against a *10* up. With literally half your available *7's* now gone *(to make 21 with)*, you should actually stand at *14!* The overall penalty for making *none* of the twelve adjustments below is about 0.04%.

Basic Strategy
SINGLE DECK blackjack

DEALER'S UP-CARD

HAND	2	3	4	5	6	7	8	9	10	A
8				dbl						
9	dbl									
11										dbl
A/2			dbl							
A/3			dbl							
A/6	dbl									
A/8					dbl					
2/2		spl								
4/4				dbl	dbl					
6/6	spl									
7/7									Std	

About one casino in five offers the surrender option. The more decks used, the more valuable surrender is. If the dealer hits *soft 17*, surrender is more valuable still, *(see Rule Variations on page 82)*.

Surrender becomes an advantage when your chance to win the hand gets down to less than 25%. Why? Imagine playing four consecutive hands with $10 riding on each one. If you lose three and win one, you're $20 behind. If you surrender all four hands, you're still $20 behind. *Winning one out of four produces the same result as surrendering all four.* But if you could win more than a fourth of those hands, you'd be better off playing them all out. And if you win less than one fourth, it'd be cheaper to just surrender them all.

Depending upon the rules and number of decks, between *three* and *seven* hands give the player less than one chance in four to win. Those hands should be surrendered in the following games.

SURRENDER
single and double deck

DEALER'S UP-CARD

HAND	10	A
15	sr	
16	sr	sr

SURRENDER
4 to 8 decks

DEALER'S UP-CARD

HAND	9	10	A
15		sr	
16	sr	sr	sr

SURRENDER
Dealer hits soft 17

DEALER'S UP-CARD

HAND	9	10	A
15		sr	sr
16	*	sr	sr
17			sr
8/8			*

*SURRENDER w/4 to 8 DECKS

That's how to play every possible starting hand with various rules and decks. The tables do **not** however, cover every hand you'll ever see. Sound like double talk? Then look at the hand on the next page.

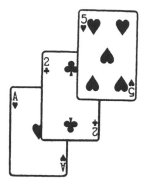

You started out with a *soft 13* against a *4* up. Basic strategy says to hit that, so you do and catch a *5* to give you a *soft 18*. Now what? Well, your chart says to double down with a *soft 18* against a *4* -- **but you can't double with three cards!** Where the charts are concerned, that one fell through the cracks.

Most players' instincts will tell them to *stand* here, and that happens to be right -- *in this particular case*. But what if your hit card was a *4*, giving you a *soft 17 (Ace/2/4)?* I often see unskilled players going both ways with this one. The right play though, is to **hit** it! So once and for all, here's the defining rule for all your *multi-card soft hands*:

A) *Never, ever stand on any kind of* **soft 17.**
B) *Hit a multi-card* **soft 18** *against a* **9, 10** *or* **Ace** *only.*

Oh, and one more thing! In a few casinos, you can double down only on *9, 10* or *11*. So where does that leave you if you can't double with say, *Ace/6* against a *5?* Then;

C) *Hit all your* **A/6's** *(or lower) and stand with all your* **A/7's** *(or higher) against a small dealer's up-card.*

COMMONLY MISPLAYED HANDS

There are certain hands that seem to be consistently misplayed, even by experienced players who consider themselves to be astute at the game. From Atlantic City to Vegas, although the faces are different, *most of the mistakes remain the same.* You've got to make sure you don't become one of those faces. Some of the most commonly misplayed hands are thoroughly discussed on the next few pages. Without having seen the basic strategy chart first, how would you have played them?

Hand	Correct Play
12 vs. **3** up	**HIT**
16 vs. **7** up	**HIT**
11 vs. **10** up	**DOUBLE**
A/3 vs. **3** up	**HIT**
A/7 vs. **3** up	**DOUBLE**
A/7 vs. **9** up	**HIT**
9,9 vs. **9** up	**SPLIT**
8,8 vs. **10** up	**SPLIT**
Blackjack vs. **A** up	**NO Even Money**

How many hands did you get wrong? The average veteran of the game misses *five* or *six!* I suspect however, that these errors are not always made out of pure ignorance. Most players know right well that they're supposed to split a pair of *8's* against any up-card. But sometimes, either because there is a big bet riding or just because he's been losing, a player breaks form and doesn't do the proper thing for fear of *"blowing"* two bets instead of one.

Also, I know that lots of players understand you're not supposed to take "even money" on your blackjack, and if quizzed about it will answer correctly. But when it comes to crunch time in the casino, they take the safe, sure way out. Many players talk a better game than they play. Don't be one of them; *it will come back to haunt you.* The explanations to the above hands are on the next few pages, and are all mathematically based.

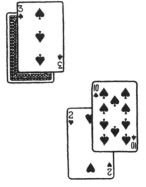

This hand is misplayed by the vast majority of players regardless of how long they've been playing blackjack. Why? I'm sure part of it's that cockeyed "*10* in-the-hole" theory. The other part probably comes from over-rating the valid principle that says you shouldn't risk busting your own hand when the dealer has a weak up-card. But think about this; when you're hitting *12*, how many cards will bust you? Four -- you're dead with any *10, Jack, Queen* or *King*. Now how many cards will give you a made hand? There are five -- any *5, 6, 7, 8* or *9* will make *17* through *21*. So more cards will make your hand than break it. Yes it's true, you should stand with *12* against a *4, 5* or *6*, but that's because of the dealer's higher bust frequency with those up-cards. With a *3* up however, the dealer isn't all that weak. She'll in fact make a hand five times out of eight! Consequently, you do a little better by hitting against a *3* than by standing.

Most players recognize that they need to hit with *16* against a *face-card*. But when the dealer has only a *7* up, many people are less intimidated and sometimes stand with that same *16*. ***This is all backwards!*** It's much more important to hit *16* against a *7* than against a *10!* Why? Let me explain -- *"The Numbers within the Numbers".*

You see, the dealer will break only 3% more often with a *7* up than with a playable *10* (26% of the time vs. 23%). And if you hit *16*, your own chance to bust is exactly the same in both cases. The problem is, against the *10,* if you manage to dodge the bullet by catching a small card like a *deuce*, you're still a solid underdog in the hand. But if you snag that same *deuce* against a *7* up, *you've probably just made yourself a winner!* Yet you had the same chance to bust in both spots.

60

Hitting *16* against a *10* a little bit like drawing to an inside straight in poker; you almost need to catch a perfect card. *16* against a *7* however is more like drawing to a flush, since there are so many more cards that'll win the hand for you. You'll learn later on in this book that there are plenty of times when you should in fact stand with *16* against a *10*. But never, ever stand with it against a *7!* You've got too many "outs" not to go for it.

This is probably the one strong double down that the most players *wimp out* on. Their major fear is that they may be doubling into a dealer's pat *20*. But did you know that when you have *11*, you'll make either *20* or *21* on your next card more often than the dealer will have a made *20*? If you both catch a *10*--you win! If you both catch a *9*, *8* or *7* -- you win! *Your* hand is the boss here! When you double down, you'll win this one six times out of eleven. You can't afford *not* to push the extra chips out there when you're a 6-to-5 favorite. Just do it!

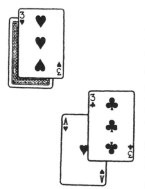

Soft hands against small up-cards are mis-played by almost everybody, everywhere. *Ace/3* against a *3* is just a generic example, and is one of many. Most players will double here and it's a horrible move! Why? Because if you just hit, you're a favorite to win. But if you double down, you drop to an even money shot and lose your edge. Lots of soft hands make good doubles-- *but this isn't one of them!* A few pages further on in this chapter, there's a complete explanation as to the "whys" and "wherefores" of soft doubling. But as a general thought, just remember this; *Ace/"tiny"* against a dealer's *"tiny"* is a bad double.

61

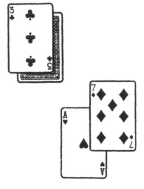

Lots of players don't want to screw around with a solid *18* here, and consequently stand. *Wrongo!* This *is* one of those many hands that makes a good soft double. That's largely because your hand is not an *Ace/"tiny"*. It's true, if you just stay pat you're a 58% shot, and if you double you're only 55%. But winning two bets 55% of the time makes more money than winning one bet 58% of the time. *(More on that in the "soft doubling" section).*

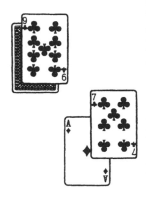

If you played an entire lifetime of blackjack and were dealt a pat *18* on every single hand, you'd die a small loser! That's the grim truth. And that dealer's *9* up there doesn't exactly help your chances any. But the *Ace* in your hand gives you some flexibility. If you stand, you'll win eight times out of twenty. If you hit all the way to a *soft 19*, a *hard 17* or bust, you'll win nine out of twenty. So take your choice -- eight wins or nine wins.

Some hands are really foolers, and this is one of them. Just as with the *soft 18* in the previous example, this *hard 18* will only beat a dealer's *9* up eight times out of twenty. But *9* against a *9* up is just a little less than an even money shot all by itself. If you're the you're the kind of player who never wants to fool with an *18*, you're playing the wrong game. You need more than *18* to win *(on average)* when the dealer's got a *9* or higher.

It may look like a *kamikaze* move, but splitting your *9's* will bring you closer to breaking even on this hand than sitting on your *18*.

16 against a *10* up is the worst blackjack situation you'll ever find yourself in. You'll win this hand 23 times out of 100 *(counting pushes as a half win and a half loss)*. But when your *16* comes in the form of a pair,

you have an escape hatch. That's because *8* against a *10* up wins 38 times out of 100. In fact, playing an *8 twice* loses less money than playing a *16 once!* That's the key. So the cheapest way out of this trap is to create two hands of *8* each, play them both and lose so much less often on each *8* that you save money in the long run. Yeah, every once in a while you'll split, lose both hands and feel like an idiot. But winning 38 hands and losing 62 twice each is still cheaper than winning 23 and losing 77 once. Do the arithmetic -- you'll see.

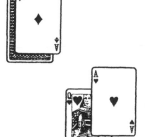

Conventional wisdom says, *"A bird in the hand is worth two in the bush"; "Don't look a gift horse in the mouth"; "Never turn down a sure thing"*. Well, clichés are cute, but they sometimes misrepresent the facts. Taking the *"even money"* guarantee on your *blackjack* when the dealer shows an *Ace* has got to be the most widespread sin committed by blackjack players anywhere. Here's why.

Let's imagine you've bet $100 on your hand and are dealt a *blackjack*. The dealer has an *Ace* up. You realize that if the dealer has anything but a *10* in the hole you'll win $150. But if she has the *10*, giving her a *blackjack* too, then you'll tie. You're also aware that if you take Insurance, you'll win $100 no matter what the dealer has. So you decide to settle for the "bird in the hand" and ask for "even money". That's when the dealer politely advises you that; *"I'm sorry sir, but we don't have the Insurance option on Tuesdays"*.

Just then, the player next to you leans over and says, *"Psst, hey Pardner; I can see you're between a rock and a hard place. So I'll tell you what I'm gonna do. I'll buy your hand from you right now for $10, win or lose. What'ya say?"*

63

*"I may have been born at night, but it wasn't just **last** night"*, you snap back. *"Unless the dealer's got a 10 in the hole, I'm about to win $150 here; and you wanna give me ten bucks? Get real!*

Now the fella comes right back with, *"Yeah, I guess you're right. Okay, I'll give you $145"*, as he slides five green chips and four reds over towards you. As quickly as you possibly can, you scoop up the $145 and wish him luck.

Well, was I correct in assuming you'd reject the $10 and accept $145? Now let me ask you, just exactly how did you arrive at those two conclusions? Maybe you can just sense intuitively that $10 is a rip-off, and $145 is a bargain, *which by the way, is true!* Well, this whole make-believe scenario was dreamed up just illustrate an important point. That point is:

THERE'S A PRICE AT WHICH IT BECOMES WORTHWHILE TO SELL YOUR HAND!

But at what price? If you shouldn't sell your hand for $10, yet you should for $145, at what price did it suddenly become worth selling? The proper way to evaluate this is to figure your average gain by playing the hand out. When you have *blackjack* and the dealer shows an *Ace*, four times out of thirteen, she will have *blackjack* too, on average. Those four times, you'll tie. The other nine times you'll win $150 for an average gain of just about $104 each. This is the *fair market value* of your hand -- $104. If you can get more than $104 for your hand, you should sell it. If you can't, *you're better off keeping it!*

When you take Insurance on your blackjack, financially it's the same as selling your hand back to the house for $100. That's too cheap, and is why they offer it at every opportunity! *By insuring a blackjack, you'll only reduce the amount of money you make on all your blackjacks combined!* If you needed a guaranteed winner that badly, you have overbet your bankroll. And if you think turning down a "sure winner" is always the wrong thing to do, you don't understand the working mechanics of profitable gambling. Don't make the mistake the house is counting on you to make. Don't sell yourself short. *Don't take "even money" on your blackjack!*

2017 Update

FOR "CHICKEN MONEY" LOVERS ONLY
Insuring a Blackjack.... *for less!*

We've just spent the last couple of pages explaining why you should *not* take even money on your blackjack. With that said, no doubt many of you will still cave in under pressure *(fearing a push)*, and you'll take the damned *"Chicken Money"* anyway. So if you are just not willing to play the hand the way you're supposed to;

THERE'S A WAY TO LOCK IN A WIN ON YOUR BLACKJACK AGAINST AN ACE WITHOUT TAKING EVEN MONEY

I want to stress that this play is not as good percentage wise as rejecting even money altogether, but it does average out more profitable than settling for the cowardly, *sure thing.* So here's what else you can do in this situation that almost nobody knows about.

Say you've got a nice $50 blackjack against the dealer's *Ace* showing. You can simply decline even money, then toss a small amount, like maybe $10 onto the Insurance ring and announce, *"For less"*. Since almost nobody ever does this, the dealer will most likely hesitate in confusion. So might the floorperson. Just explain that you're taking Insurance for less, the same as you could if you had a *20*, or any other hand. It's perfectly legal, and after they scratch their heads, they're going to have to let you do it.

Now, one of two things will happen. Usually the dealer won't have blackjack and she'll take your $10 Insurance *loser,* then pay you $75 for your winning blackjack – a $65 profit. But about 30% of the time, she'll have the *10* underneath and your blackjack will push. Those times, she'll pay you $20 for your Insurance *winner.*

What you've done here is skirt around the possibility of getting nothing for your blackjack. Sometimes you'll make only 20 bucks, but usually you'll net the $65. The real point however, is rather than collecting $50 every time, you'll now "average" a bit over $51 per time -- and you never had to settle for a total push!

Still, it must be pointed out that simply declining even money here would produce an averaged profit of nearly $52. So take your pick -- $50, $51 or $52. But remember, blackjack is a game of very close percentages. Give away $1 here, $2 there and a little more along the way, and pretty soon you're dead meat! *I'm just sayin'* .

THE QUESTION OF SPLITTING *"Fs"*

There's an ancient blackjack adage that says, *"Never split anything that starts with an F"*. The "F" stands *for Fours, Fives* and *Faces*. Blackjack adages are a dime a dozen. This adage is part right and part wrong. So let's clear it up.

First, the adage is 100% right in that nobody should ever split a pair of *Fives*. Always play *5/5* the same way as *6/4, 7/3* or *8/2.*

Next, a plain basic strategy player should never split *Faces*. The card counting section of this book explains those rare times when splitting *10s **can be*** an expert play. But it's not for amateurs.

Now for that last "F", a pair of *Fours*. This hand confounds many. Often when someone is dealt *4/4* against a so-called "bust card", he'll instinctively grab some extra chips, then pause and think. He feels compelled to do something extra – but what?

DOUBLE DOWN?? – Ask yourself this: If you had a *5/3* or a *6/2* against a "bust card", would you double down with those? *You Should Not (except in single deck)!* For doubling with two to eight decks, a *5/3, 6/2* and *4/4* are all the same hand! ***Don't do it!***

HIT?? – If doubling isn't right, then what about just hitting your total of *8?* Well, with poor rules that would be the best thing.

SPLIT?? – If it seems like a lame idea to split up a *moderate* start of *8* into two *inferior* starts of *4* each, then think about this;

WHAT IF YOU SPLIT *4/4* AND CATCH A
5, 6, 7 OR *ACE* ON EITHER *4?*

If the rules allow you to *double-after-split*, and most games do, any of those catches will give you a profitable double down *against a 5 or a 6!* Many times you'll catch a double on one *4* and pull a third *4* on the other one, enabling you to extend the chain out to three or more hands. *Splitting your 4s against a 5 or 6 will give you one or more doubles or re-splits over 60% of the time!* That's why the correct play for a pair of *4s* with two or more decks is:

❖ *As long as the rules allow you to double-after-split, then split your 4s against a dealer's 5 or 6 only.*

❖ *If you can't "DAS", then just hit the hand the same as you would with 5/3 or 6/2 (see charts on pages 54 & 55)*

64.2

FOLLOWING THROUGH

So now you know your basic strategy like the back of your hand, right? Not so fast! You can still get caught off guard and make some unexpected mistakes when surprise situations pop up and catch you by surprise. Here's what I mean:

Not Re-Splitting: Suppose you have a pair of *8's* against a dealer's *10* up. You hate your hand, but grit your teeth, put another bet out there and split. Now you catch a third *8!* What should you do? Well, every time you split and "re-pair", you have the same situation you faced a second ago. You can either play a new total of *16* or convert it into two more *8's*. If breaking up the first two *8's* was the most cost-efficient play, then splitting this new pair is the best move again! You may not like the revolting situation you've fallen into, but like it or not you're in it -- and re-splitting is always the best way out.

That'll work in your favor sometimes too, like when you split two *9's* against a *6* for example. The more *9's* you catch here, the better you like it! Never moan to yourself thinking, *"Oh no, not another one!"* You should be so lucky as to have *9* against a *6* on every hand for the rest of your life! Fire those chips out there!

Forgetting to Double: Not following through strikes in other forms as well. Look at the following scenario:

You split a pair of *7's* against a *4* up. On your first *7*, you catch a *6* and stand with *13*. On your second *7* you buy another *7*, re-split and catch an *8*, standing disgustedly with *15*. Now on your third *7* you catch a *deuce* giving you a total of *9*. ***Don't forget to double down if the rules allow "double after splits!"*** Never let the fact that you already have two bad hands slow you down one iota! Would you rather save that extra bet for your next blind hand? Heck no! This is the one where you have the edge -- *right now!*

Multi-Card Brain Lock: Here's one more subtle form of not following through:

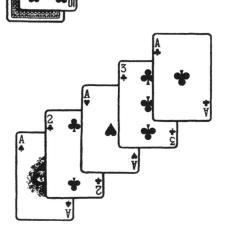

You're dealt an *Ace/2* against a dealer's *face-card*, hit and catch another *Ace*. So you hit again, buying a *3*, then take a third hit catching yet another *Ace*. When you see you've finally reached *18*, you might be so relieved that you'll instinctively wave the dealer off. ***But you must hit a soft 18 against a 9, 10 or Ace!*** Don't let these unexpected developments catch you off guard. Stay alert and never soften up on your discipline.

Now, how much can *not* following through with all your basic strategy cost you when you play blackjack??

**IF YOU NEVER RE-SPLIT A PAIR, NEVER DOUBLE
AFTER A SPLIT AND NEVER HIT A MULTI-CARD
HARD 16 OR A MULTI-CARD SOFT 18** (that you
should); **IT'LL ADD** $^1/3$% **TO THE HOUSE EDGE**

Just failing to follow all the way through will put your net
disadvantage up to around $^8/10$% in a shoe game even if you do
everything else right.

---

*So much for specific problem hands in blackjack. Now let's focus
on one generic hand group that spells "trouble" to most players.*

SOFT DOUBLES

It's just a blackjack fact of life. Whether it be not hitting
enough, not doubling enough or doubling too much, nearly all
players bungle their *soft* hands. As a playing aid, remember this
fundamental soft hand rule:

**THE BEST WAY TO HANDLE SOFT HANDS IS
TO ALWAYS COUNT YOUR ACE AS 11 FIRST**

-- *until doing so would bring your total over 21.* Then revert the
value of the *Ace* back to *1* and play your cards like the *hard* hand
it has become.

The real problem for nearly all players however, is their
soft double downs. That's when you double against a small up-
card with an *Ace* and a small or medium card in your hand. For
the typical blackjack player, this is the very least understood
category of hands -- and the very last to be learned.

When I first started playing blackjack and saw other
players doubling on soft hands, I thought to myself, *"What the
heck is the idea behind that?"*

Well, basically the idea behind any blackjack maneuver is
to play the hand in such a way as to provide the maximum return
on your wager. First off, in order for *any* kind of doubling down

67

to be beneficial you must be more likely to win the hand than lose it. Otherwise, why would you be jacking up your bet?

But just being a favorite on the hand isn't enough to make doubling down the right play. Doubling down must also return a greater profit than playing that hand *any other way!* With many soft hands against a weak dealer's up-card, you make money over time regardless of whether you hit or double. But with some of them, just hitting it makes *more* money *(since it saves you the right to take a second hit when your first hit is too small)!* In some cases you even go from an odds-on favorite to an underdog when you double down rather than hit. *So you've got to know what you're doing when you start doubling down with a soft hand.*

Proper soft doubling can gain the basic strategy player about 0.10% in six deck play, and a tad more with fewer decks. But many overly-aggressive players tend to double down with almost any soft hand against any small up-card. In fact, *I think many players give more back to the house in bad soft doubles than they gain in good ones!* Take a look at the two hands below:

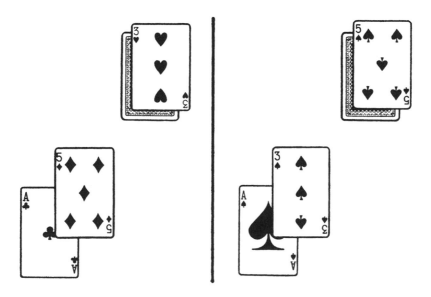

They appear pretty similar, don't they? To the majority of players, these two hands look just about the same for playing purposes.

Well they're not! *Ace/5* against a *3* becomes a small underdog if you double it; but *Ace/3* vs. *5* is a solid favorite and a good double.

DON'T DO LIKE SO MANY OTHERS WHO PLAY THEIR SOFT DOUBLES BACKWARDS!

The typical ham'n-egger wants to double with a hand like *Ace/2* against a *3* all day long, but won't double with *Ace/7* against that same *3* up. He doesn't want to tamper with a made hand *(the soft 18)*. Fact is, doubling with *Ace/6* and *Ace/7* are your biggest soft double moneymakers! Here's the key reason why.

If you double down with that *Ace/2*, how many cards can you buy that will give you a made hand? Think about it. There are only **five**. Just a *4, 5, 6, 7* or *8* will give you *17* through *21*. The other **eight** cards all leave you with *12* through *16* – a *stiff*. Now you need the dealer to break, or you lose! You've also got exactly the same poor chance to make a hand when you double with *Ace/3, Ace/4* or *Ace/5*.

But as soon as you reach *Ace/6,* it's the other way around! **Eight** cards will now make you a hand and only **five** cards leave you stiff. Because of that, you've got to be against a very weak dealer's up-card to double with *Ace/2* through *Ace/5*, but should be more aggressive with *Ace/6* and *Ace/7*.

To do things right, you should soft double down in *eighteen* specific situations where you have *Ace/2* through *Ace/7* against a small dealer's up-card. But which ones? It can get pretty confusing looking at all those zig-zag steps in your basic strategy chart. So to zone you in on the right moves, just use these next three simple rules of thumb as your guide. They're practically a no-brainer to play; the only time you have to think is when the dealer's up-card is a *3* or a *4*. Using this guide will get you to pull the trigger correctly on seventeen of the eighteen hands.

> 1) *Never soft double against a deuce.*
> (when playing standard basic strategy)
>
> 2) *Always soft double against a 5 or 6.*
>
> 3) *When the dealer has a 3 or 4 up,*
>   *play by the "RULE of 9".*

69

Now what'n blazes is the *Rule of 9?* Simply add the dealer's up-card to your kicker *(the card next to your Ace).* If they total *9* or more, double down! If it's less, just hit. The following example should make the *Rule of 9* crystal clear.

JOE   **JENNY**

Since the dealer has a *3* or *4* up, the "Rule of 9" applies. So before acting, Joe adds his own *5* to the dealer's *3*. Since that equals only *8*, he should *not* double but just hit. However, Jenny's *6* plus the dealer's *3* equal *9*, thus she *should* double down. Got it?

And as for that 18th hand not covered by these three rules? You should also just *barely* double with *Ace/4* against a *4* – but it's a real *hairline* double. If you always simply hit that one, it'll take less than one thousandth of a percent off your overall game.

Dealer's Bust-out Rate: Notice throughout the strategy charts how there's a fairly distinct line of demarcation between the dealer having a *6* for an up-card and a *7* up. That's because with a small up-card she'll have to draw to get to *17*, and may bust while trying. But with a *7* or higher, she's apt to be pat. As a player, the first thing you should notice while the cards are being dealt is the dealer's up-card, even before you look at your own hand. It sets the stage for how you will play your cards.

After all is said and done, the dealer will bust 28% of the time. But you can gauge her chances more closely by noting her up-card. The following chart lists the dealer's chance to bust in a multi-deck game depending upon her specific up-card *(bust-out rates for single deck are for practical purposes, virtually the same).*

DEALER'S BUST-OUT RATE
(when showing a.........)

2	3	4	5	6	7	8	9	10	Ace
35%	37%	40%	42%	42%	26%	24%	23%	23%	17%

These percentages apply to those occasions when the dealer does *not* have blackjack. If she did, you wouldn't even get to play your hand out. Notice the profound drop between the *6* and the *7*. This is why the strategies diverge so greatly there. Also if the dealer must hit a *soft 17,* even though she generally helps her hand she now has a chance to bust it. As a result, her bust-out rate with a *6* up will increase to nearly **44%**, and to about **20%** with an *Ace* up.

Notice by the way, that there is absolutely *no* up-card with which the dealer will break as often as she'll make a hand. So by definition, the dealer *never* has a "bust card" up.

2017 Update

HOW OFTEN SHOULD THE DEALER BUST A STIFF ?

Once the dealer turns over her hole card and she actually does have *12* thru *16,* her chances to bust now go way up. Mind you.... *a dealer's 5 showing does not mean she has 15!*

The following list tells you the dealer's chances to bust her stiff hands in multi-deck play. Figures are for a two-card starting hand. Busting multi-card stiffs such as *4/5/5* or *2/3/4/3* can be 1% higher, since they take more hand-saving small cards out of play.

Dealer Has:	12	13	14	15	16.
Chance to Bust:	48%	52%	55%	58%	61%

Notice that these bust-out figures are quite a bit different than just looking at a *2* through *6* up. The dealer is now favored to bust every stiff except *12.*

WHAT HAPPENS WHEN THE DEALER HITS A SOFT 17?

When this book was first written back in 2002, it was fairly common for the dealer to *stand* on *soft 17*. But here in 2017, most low and medium stakes games have gone to *hitting soft 17*.

Given a choice, you'd rather they just stand on all *17s*. Their hitting it sometimes helps you and sometimes hurts. But at the bottom line, the house gains $^2/_{10}\%$ in *hit soft 17* games. Here's a nutshell picture of how that all shakes out with a multi-deck shoe.

NO CHANGE: About **35** out of each 100 times the dealer hits a *soft 17,* she'll either pull a *10*, or take multiple hits that add up to 10 *(as with A/6 – 5-3-2)*. These all make a *hard 17* and don't matter.

DEALER IMPROVES: Another **44** times out of 100, the dealer will catch cards either on her first hit *(i.e. 6/A – 2)*, or on later hits that improve her total to *18* thru *21*. Those will sting the most when she makes the strong hand on her second time around after developing a stiff *(such as with 6/A – 6-3-4)*.

DEALER BUSTS: If there's a bright side to the dealer hitting *soft 17*, it's that she now has a chance to bust it. This gift from the gambling gods will drop into your lap an average of **21** times out of 100 *(like when A/6 – 7-10 happens)*.

So of the 65 times that there's a change in the dealer's total by hitting a *soft 17;*

Dealer Improves	**44 times**
Dealer Busts	**21 times**

Those lopsided odds will be working against you once every 56 hands. That's how often the dealer will have, or build some kind of *soft 17*. Remember, she *will* hit on hands like *A/2 – 4* and even oddball stuff like *A/2 – A-2-A*. Over the whole game though, the net difference boils down to $^2/_{10}\%$.

So then, can this extra house edge blackball a blackjack game altogether? It's not a good thing, but it *is* tolerable. It'll almost never make the difference between a winning or losing day, but it *will* cost a $20 bettor about $4 per hour over time.

2017 Update

WHY SHOULD I HIT MY SOFT 18??

Here's a fact. An *18* is a decisive underdog against a dealer's *9, 10* or *Ace*. So when you're dealt an *Ace/7* in that spot, what'ya gonna' do? Most players instinctively reason that, "*Only 3 cards help the hand, 4 cards will keep it the same and the other 6 cards all make it worse.*" So they persistently wave off the *18*.

On the surface, that may seem logical. *But they're only thinking as far as their first hit!* It's true, if you hit your *soft 18* you'll improve it on your first hit only 23 times out of 100.

But you'll also make 38 *stiffs (12s thru 16s)* along the way. And those *stiffs* — you'll keep on hitting! When you do, you'll improve your stiff to *19* or better *10 more times out of the 38.* By the time you finish hitting 100 hands, on average you'll make:

> a hard **18**..............**34** times
> **17** or **bust**............**32½** times
> **19** thru **21**..............**33½** times

In the end, you actually help the hand a little more often than you hurt it! That difference might seem trivial. But there's an *extra* reason to hit your *soft 18* against a dealer's *9, 10* or *Ace* because:

WHEN YOU HELP THAT *18* YOUR CHANCES TO WIN GO UP, <u>MORE</u> THAN THEY GO DOWN WHEN YOU HURT IT

Here's a case in point: If you stand with your *soft 18* against an *Ace**, you'll win **5** hands out of **13**. If you hit all 13 and turn them all into *17s*, you'll win only **3** hands. But if you make all *19s* you'll win **8** hands. *Overall, more wins are gained by improving the hand than are lost by worsening it.* Those two differences when you hit, combine together to yield the following bottom line results:

YOU HAVE	DEALER SHOWS			
Ace/7	**9**	**10**	**A***	**A****
WIN IF YOU STAND	41%	41%	39%	45%
WIN IF YOU HIT	45%	43%	42%	45½%

Note: all ties count as ½ win & ½ loss.   *hits soft 17   **stands soft 17

So the next time you're dealt a *soft 18* against a dealer's *9, 10* or *Ace – just hit it,* as per the basic strategy chart on page 54.

71.2

INSURANCE

Taking Insurance, *aka* "even money" when you have blackjack has already been discussed in great detail. *Don't take it!* But what about at other times? The answer is -- you should *practically* never take it! Why not? Because Insurance is basically a bad all around bet *(remember the Basic Principle of Profitable Gambling from page 10).*

For every 13 times the dealer shows an *Ace,* she'll have a *10* in the hole just about 4 times. If you made a $5 Insurance bet on 13 different hands against her *Ace* showing and she had blackjack 4 times, you'd win 4 Insurance bets of $10 each *(2-to-1 payoff odds).* Then you'd go on to lose $5 the other 9 times for a $5 net loss on the 13 hands combined. *This is just a small cross-section of what would happen in the long run for all the times you took Insurance.*

"But what about protecting my hand?", you ask. What makes you think you can protect your hand?? You've got to get that kind of thinking out of your head! Now, read this next statement twice!

YOU'LL ALWAYS WIN OR LOSE THE BET ON YOUR HAND JUST THE SAME WHETHER YOU TOOK INSURANCE OR NOT

If you insure an *18* and the dealer turns up blackjack, your *18* is still going to lose! You'll then win your Insurance bet to break even on the two wagers combined. But they were two separate bets, one *fair* and one *bad.* Linking the two outcomes together in your mind will mislead you into thinking that the *bad* bet is a *good* bet!

Insurance offers 2-to-1 payoff odds on a bet that is normally $2^{1}/_{4}$-to-1 against winning. So if you had no bet riding on any hand, would you want to make an Insurance bet based on its own merit? No – that would be a sucker bet! Well, just having a hand in front of you doesn't make the Insurance bet any better. *The outcome on your hand itself won't change, and you'll still lose money on all the Insurance bets you make over time!* So always think, *"big picture"* and ignore any Insurance *unless* you know something "privy" about the remaining cards. That comes a little later in this book.

INSURE A GOOD HAND???

Most players will never insure a bad hand, but many still believe in insuring a good one, like *20* for example. They feel that if the dealer has blackjack, they avoid losing money with a strong hand. And without a blackjack, the dealer will have a hard time trying to beat your *20*. But the truth is, all things being equal, *20* would be the *worst* possible hand to insure! The reason is, in order to win the Insurance bet the dealer has to have a *10* in the hole. But your *20* just took two *10's* out of play *(presuming you don't have Ace/9)*. Now the Insurance bet, which is a bad bet to begin with has just gotten worse! Here's the thing.

  The instant you're dealt *20* against an *Ace* up, you're a solid favorite to make money. You're in a *positive* situation even though you could lose to a blackjack. But if you decide to insure your *20*, you're accepting 2-to-1 odds on a new, second bet that is now probably 2.3-to-1 against winning. That adds a negative element to your position.

  If combining both those bets together seems like it produces a net advantage, that's because it does. But the entire source of your edge came from being dealt your *20* in the first place! The Insurance part just drags down the overall value of your favorable position. In gambling, *you should never make a bad bet in an effort to protect a good one!* The best thing to do is just live or die with the good bet. Want to see all of that a little clearer? We'll say you're a high roller playing two spots for $1000 apiece and are dealt the two hands in the picture below:

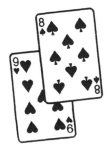

73

Believing it's smart to insure a good hand, you immediately toss $500 out towards the Insurance ring. The dealer then places the chips right on the line, but closer to the *17* than the *20*.

"*No, no!*" you panic. "*I want to insure the 20 -- not the 17!* Silly you! Don't you realize that it makes absolutely no difference which of the two hands you insure? You're going to come out if it with exactly the same financial result whether you insure the *20* or the *17!* That's right.

If you insure the *20* and the dealer has blackjack, you're going to lose $1000 on your *17* and break even on your *20*. Net result -- minus $1000, right? But what if you were a total lamebrain and actually insured the *17* instead? Now you're going to break even on your *17* and lose $1000 on the *20* -- *still netting the same $1000 loss.* Simple enough?

Okay, so what if the dealer doesn't have blackjack and ends up busting? If you insure the *20*, you'll net $500 there and win another $1000 on the *17* for a $1500 net profit. And if you were goofy enough to insure the *17* instead, you'll net $500 there and win $1000 on your *20*. *Both ways, you make 1500 bucks!* Let's keep going.

Finally, how would things come out if the dealer makes, say *18?* Well, insuring your *20* you'd net a $500 profit on that hand, then lose $1000 on your *17* for a combined loss of $500. But if you did it back-asswards and insured the *17*, you'd lose $1500 on it, then win $1000 on your *20* -- *for the same $500 combined loss.*

Is it sinking in? No matter what the dealer has or makes, your end result comes out the same whether you insure the *20* or the *17!* That's because Insurance is not a bet on *your* hand -- it's a bet on the *dealer's* hand! Lots of players think that insuring a *20* is smart and insuring a *17* is stupid - when in reality;

BOTH PLAYS ARE STUPID!

So the next time you see some goofball insuring his *13*, remember, he's no dumber than you are for insuring your *20*.

DOUBLING FOR LESS

It's surprising how creative some gamblers can get at the *"21"* tables. Unfortunately, blackjack is not a game that lends itself well to spontaneous creativity. Some players go far beyond the call of gamesmanship to find ways to hurt themselves while playing blackjack.

One of the most illogical maneuvers there are is *doubling down for less than twice the original bet.* It usually seems to occur when a player is psychologically torn between hitting and doubling with his hand.

You need to remember that when you double down, you're making a trade-off with the house. In exchange for the right to double your wager after having already seen your hand, you're giving up the right to take additional cards if you don't like your first hit. This will usually decrease how often you win the hand, but still increase your net gain due to the extra action you've put in as an odds-on favorite. But;

**IF YOU DON'T PUT THE MAXIMUM AMOUNT
UP, YOU'RE NOT TAKING FULL ADVANTAGE
OF YOUR END OF THE BARGAIN!**

As an example, let's take the case where you've made a $15 wager and are dealt;

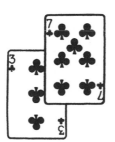

If you just hit this hand, you'll win it 60 times out of 100 *(counting pushes as a half win and a half loss)*. But if you double down you'll win only 57 times *(again, adjusting for pushes)*, because if you catch something like a stupid *3*, you're stuck with *13* against the dealer's *8*.

Nevertheless, doubling down is still the right play because winning 57 hands and losing 43 at $30 each makes a $420 profit; where winning 60 and losing 40 at $15 each nets only $300. This exemplifies the principle that *the most likely way to win the hand is not necessarily the best play.*

But, what would happen if you "doubled for less" by putting only an extra $5 chip up next to your original $15 wager in that same situation? It might seem like a compromise, but it's not!

Add it up. Now you're going to go 57 and 43 at $20 apiece for a total gain of only $280. That's the worst of all three worlds! And it works that way because *you're shrinking your edge on the hand without maximizing the size of your bet!* So never, ever shoot yourself in the foot by doubling for less.

WOULDA' SHOULDA' COULDA'

Please do everybody a big favor. Don't be one of those players who constantly second guesses everyone else's moves. That can't help you one bit. Here's a common, every day example;

Like a typical amateur, first base stands with *12* against a *3*. Center field correctly doubles down and buys a *10*, then the rookie at third base hits his *13* and busts with a *9*. The dealer turns over a *Jack* in the hole, then promptly pulls a *7* for a total of *20!*

First base immediately pounds the table in anger, objecting that if everybody *woulda'* just stayed pat the dealer *woulda'* busted with center field's *10*. Center field argues right back that his double on *soft 18* was the proper play and that third base *shoulda'* stood pat, which *woulda'* saved the breaking *9* for the dealer. Third base defiantly points out that he's gambling with his own money and can play his own hand any *effing* way he pleases. Does any of this sound familiar?

It goes on all the time and it's such a waste! What good can it possibly do to notice what *woulda'* happened if everybody did what they *shoulda'*? Is basing your next decision upon the most recent result a winning strategy? No -- it's not!

Here's what I mean. Just suppose that when third base hit his *13*, the next two cards came out in reverse order. That is, the *7* came first *(instead of the 9)* giving him *20*. Then the *9* came second *(instead of the 7)* to break the dealer? What lesson could you possibly learn from that?

Should you then start hitting all your *13's* against a *3* from third base to force the dealer to break? Or would the message be to stand with *12* against a *3* from first base when there's a bad player at third? Of course they're both bad plays, so taking any pointers from their results can only mislead you. The reality is, *you never know which way the cards will change if somebody alters their play*. So the best thing for you to do is just to;

KNOW YOUR CORRECT PLAY IN ADVANCE, MAKE IT AND NEVER LOOK BACK

Quarterbacking the hand after it's over is the easiest thing in the world to do. Unless you can tell everybody how the cards are going to come out *before they do*, your post mortems are not only senseless, but irritating. So please -- forget about all the *"woulda', shoulda', coulda's!*

PLAYER'S HAND ODDS

Now that you understand correct basic blackjack strategy, you know just what to expect whenever you hit, double or split, right? Not really. The vast majority of gamblers grossly underestimate the swings that come with short and mid-term *luck*. Math guys call it *variance*. In blackjack, variance means you're dealing with a shoe full of about 300 shuffled cards, and although that does create their odds – *anything can still happen today.*

SOLID FAVORITES: It can become painfully obvious when you have an awesome looking *11* against a wimpy *6* up. You gotta' double it; you're way ahead of the dealer! But all too often you catch a baby, and she pulls a four card *20. "How do they do it?"*, you gripe; *"I'm supposed to win that one! What's going on here?"*

Well, what's going on is you *are* supposed to win that one – *two* times out of *three!* That last part's the key. You might lose that hand three straight times today, but you'll win it six times some other day. This is the erratic nature of short term gambling.

BIG UNDERDOGS: How about when you hit *15* against a *10?* You should lose that one 75% of the time. But if you win it, you'll likely dismiss it as a natural by-product of your skillful play. Yet the truth is, sometimes you get lucky -- and sometimes you don't.

Following is a list of 60 run-of-the-mill hands and their rounded odds of being won by the player *(counting pushes as a ½ win and a ½ loss). All odds assume proper basic strategy play.* An 8-to-5 favorite means it should win just about 80 times for every 50 times it loses. As for this one time? *It's a gamble.* But the odds will give you a clear picture of what to expect *over the long haul.*

Notice from the list how you're an underdog with some hands that might feel like favorites – such as *Ace/5* against a *2,* or *17* vs. *5.* If it was easy to win hands like that, *the game wouldn't be there!*

"IFFY" PAIRS: Also notice how proper pair splits make you either a bigger favorite or a smaller underdog. With *9/9* against an *8* for instance, each *9* is as much a favorite over the dealer's *8* as your *18* is -- so splitting just multiplies your edge! And with the dreaded *8/8* against a *10,* your *16* is so bad that you're actually a smaller overall financial underdog by putting up a second bet to play *two hands* of *8* against a *10! Don't wimp out on these splits.*

HAND	PLAYER'S ODDS
20 vs. **8** up	**8**-to-**1** favorite
20 vs. **6** up	**11**-to-**2** favorite
20 vs. **4** up	**5**-to-**1** favorite
20 vs. **2** up	**9**-to-**2** favorite
19 vs. **A** up*	**9**-to-**5** favorite *(S17)*; **3**-to-**2** w/*H17*
19 vs. **10** up*	**8**-to-**7** favorite
19 vs. **9** up	**9**-to-**5** favorite
19 vs. **7** up	**4**-to-**1** favorite
19 vs. **2** up	**11**-to-**5** favorite
18 vs. **A** up*	**6**-to-**5** underdog *(S17)*; **8**-to-**5** w/ *H17*
18 vs. **10** up*	**7**-to-**5** underdog
A/7 vs. **10** up*	**4**-to-**3** underdog
18 vs. **9** up	**3**-to-**2** underdog
A/7 vs. **9** up	**6**-to-**5** underdog
18 vs. **8** up	**6**-to-**5** favorite
9/9 vs. **8** up	**6**-to-**5** favorite *on each hand***
18 vs. **7** up	**11**-to-**5** favorite
18 vs. **5** up	**3**-to-**2** favorite
18 vs. **2** up	**5**-to-**4** favorite
17 vs. **10** up*	**12**-to-**5** underdog
17 vs. **9** up	**5**-to-**2** underdog
17 vs. **7** up	**5**-to-**4** underdog
A/6 vs. **7** up	**11**-to-**10** favorite
17 vs. **5** up	**11**-to-**10** underdog
17 vs. **2** up	**7**-to-**5** underdog
A/6 vs. **2** up	Even Money
16 vs. **A** up*	**16**-to-**5** underdog *(S17)*; **17**-to-**5** w/*H17*
16 vs. **10** up*	**17**-to-**5** underdog
8/8 vs. **10** up*	**8**-to-**5** underdog *on each hand***
16 vs. **9** up	**15½**-to-**5** underdog
16 vs. **7** up	**12**-to-**5** underdog
16 vs. **5** up	**7**-to-**5** underdog
15 vs. **10** up*	**15½**-to-**5** underdog
15 vs. **8** up	**5**-to-**2** underdog
15 vs. **4** up	**3**-to-**2** underdog
14 vs. **2** up	**9**-to-**5** underdog
7/7 vs. **2** up	**7**-to-**6** underdog *on each hand***
13 vs. **8** up	**8**-to-**5** underdog
13 vs. **2** up	**9**-to-**5** underdog
12 vs. **5** up	**7**-to-**5** underdog
12 vs. **4** up	**3**-to-**2** underdog
12 vs. **3** up	**8**-to-**5** underdog
6/6 vs. **3** up	**9**-to-**8** underdog *on each hand***
11 vs. **10** up*	**6**-to-**5** favorite *x 2 bets*
11 vs. **6** up	**2**-to-**1** favorite *x 2 bets*
11 vs. **2** up	**8**-to-**5** favorite *x 2 bets*
10 vs. **9** up	**7**-to-**6** favorite *x 2 bets*
10 vs. **6** up	**9**-to-**5** favorite *x 2 bets*
10 vs. **2** up	**3**-to-**2** favorite *x 2 bets*
9 vs. **9** up	**10**-to-**9** underdog
9 vs. **8** up	**6**-to-**5** favorite
9 vs. **3** up	**8**-to-**7** favorite *x 2 bets*
8 vs. **6** up	**5**-to-**4** favorite
4/4 vs. **6** up	**6**-to-**5** favorite *on each hand***
A/7 vs. **3** up	**6**-to-**5** favorite *x 2 bets*
A/3 vs. **5** up	**8**-to-**7** favorite *x 2 bets*
A/5 vs. **3** up	Even Money
A/2 vs. **5** up	**8**-to-**7** favorite *x 2 bets*
A/2 vs. **2** up	**11**-to-**10** favorite
A/5 vs. **2** up	**21**-to-**20** underdog

*After dealer checks hole card and does **not** have blackjack. ** w/ double after split allowed

79

LEARN TO TRUST THE ODDS

When I was first learning to play blackjack back in the mid-'70's, there were several plays in the basic strategy that didn't look right to me. A *soft 18* against a *9* was a classic example. Taking a hit with *18* just went against my grain. Every time this hand came up, I stuttered and stammered. I simply *didn't trust the odds.*

The least I could do to satisfy myself was to deal the hand out 1000 times, standing on the first 500 and hitting the second 500. I still have that tally sheet in my old blackjack notebook. Here are the results;

	STANDING	HITTING
Win	173	201
Lose	267	247
Push	60	52

That was good enough for me -- *I never stood with that hand again!* I also learned to trust the odds on a number of other questionable hands through similar exercises. Was I reinventing the wheel? Not really. Then what's my point?

EVERY SERIOUS BLACKJACK PLAYER MUST DO WHAT'S NECESSARY TO REMOVE ANY DOUBT WHICH MAY CAUSE HIM TO DO THE WRONG THING UNDER PRESSURE

This can extend beyond the scope of merely testing out the basic strategy. For instance, do you really believe all that "goody goody" crap about the dealer having a *10* in the hole only 30% of the time? Then how come whenever she has a *10* up, she always seems to have *20* -- huh?? For that matter, why the hell does the dealer seem to have a *10* up so often?

Some years ago, I went through a killer losing spell. If I was dealt a *20* against the dealer's *10* up, it seemed we always pushed. Besides that, I'd gotten punch-drunk from constantly having a dealer's *10* in my face. I became so gun-shy that I just expected to get beat, even with a good hand! *"Are things really on the level in this game?"* I began to ask myself.

For me, there was only one thing to do. I vowed not to play blackjack again until I had completed a little experiment. So for my next eight or ten hours in the casinos, I just circled the tables, taking data. What sort of data? In a six deck game, we know that when the dealer doesn't have blackjack, 95 cards out of 287 will give her another *10* in the hole making a pat *20*. That would be only 33.1% of the time. It seemed more like 70% or 80% to me -- *how about you?*

So I walked from table to table and recorded 1000 situations where the dealer had a *playable 10* up. He/she turned out to have another *10* in the hole 341 of those times. That was pretty darned close the theoretical 331 figure and a far cry from 700 or 800!

Hmm, which figure was I to believe -- a carefully recorded 1000 hand record, or my perceived recollection of my overall past? I decided that the pain associated with losing had probably caused me to remember mostly, *those hands which had hurt me.*

So I began to play again with an open mind, and this time became genuinely surprised at how often I noticed that the dealer did *not* have a *10* underneath his/her *10* up! Mystically, it almost seemed like a new game! Soon after, that vicious losing streak, like all other streaks came to an end.

The lesson is this. We all go through negative swan dives. At those times, our convictions will be tested. You cannot afford to become tentative and start de-optimizing your play. That will only lead to beating yourself.

When you have the edge on a situation, you must fire the extra chips out there relentlessly, such as with *11* against a *10*, even if you've been getting *buried* all day! If you lose -- *you just plain lose!* And if you're not too sure about hitting that *7/6/A/A/A* against a *7* up, play it out a few hundred times at home on your kitchen table until you're convinced.

YOU'LL NEVER GROW BEYOND THE STATUS OF A FRUSTRATED LOSER IF YOU DON'T LEARN TO TRUST THE ODDS

WHAT 6-TO-5 BLACKJACK DOES TO YOUR CHANCES

Back around the turn of this century, a few casinos began to bring back single deck *21,* but paid only 6-to-5 on blackjack. In the original edition of this book, one small paragraph in Chapter 11 cautioned players briefly about this vastly inferior hybrid.

Sadly since then, 6-to-5 blackjack games have begun to sprout up in today's standard shoe games, mostly at entry level stakes. Many people play casually enough that they just don't care, or don't understand how much it hurts them. A common brush-off remark is, *"What's the big deal? I never get blackjack anyway".* So in this 2017 update, I'll try harder to explain what the big deal is.

Whether you think you ever get blackjack or not, you'll in fact receive an average of one natural every 21 hands over your playing lifetime. Say you play for five hours at $10 per hand. At a four handed table, you'll likely have 21 blackjacks over that period. One of them will figure to push with the dealer's own blackjack. Then you'll be paid $12 apiece on the other 20 blackjacks instead of the full $15, and the house will have shorted your chip stack by $60! That alone will shift your *daily win/loss range* downward.

Now suppose you're a solid basic strategy player who faces a 0.64% house advantage in a regular 3-to-2 blackjack game that hits on soft *17.* On *average,* your five hour session would've cost you $28. But with 6-to-5 blackjack, their house edge will now be a full 2% and you'll *average* a loss of 88 bucks! Do that once a month, and by the end of the year you'll now *probably* be down over $1000 rather than $300 or $350 had blackjacks paid 3-to-2!

Those are just the *averages.* Lady Luck will have her part in what *really* happens. So here's a chart that merely tells how your *chances* get affected by switching from 3-to-2 blackjack to 6-to-5.

Blackjack Payoff	*Standard Daily Win / Loss Range	Avg. Daily Result	Average Year	Statistical Odds Against a Winning Year
3-to-2	+$210 to -$265	-$28	-$330	2 to 1
6-to-5	+$150 to -$325	-$88	-$1050	9 to 1

That's how the 6-to-5 payoff grinds away at your odds. If you play once a year, not that big a deal. But for repeat players, *it's murder!*

6-to-5 Strategy Adjustments

If you ever do get sucked into playing 6-to-5 blackjack, then **take even money on blackjack against an Ace....***if they'll give it to you!* Many 6-to-5 games don't allow even money because at such lousy payoff odds, even money becomes the right play! On a $10 blackjack with 6-to-5 odds, just waiting it out would *average* you only **$8.31** per time -- where even money always gets the full **$10**. If even money is not allowed, **do not take Insurance on your blackjack**! Insurance will reduce your *averaged* payback to just **$7.92** per time.

CAUTION: *Don't get cute by doubling down on blackjack* to make up for the 6-to-5 payoff. Even against a lowly 6 up, doubling wins just two times out of three! If you double a $10 blackjack three times, win two and lose one, you're **$20** ahead. Just taking the $12 payoff all three times puts you **$36** ahead!

2017 Update

AN OVERVIEW OF BLACKJACK SIDE BETS

Twenty or thirty years ago, blackjack was just blackjack. But today, casinos are boosting their blackjack profits with side bets that carry bigger house edges than their edge on blackjack itself.

Many of these side bets are owned by outside businesses who partner with the casino in exchange for royalties or fees. Side bets are mathematically designed to win enough *extra* money to make up for fewer hands dealt per hour, cover fees to the side bet partner, and still have something left over to increase overall net table profit. It's not a mechanism that bodes well for the player.

It's true, a few side bets have appeared that can be exploited for profit, but most are just plain sucker bets. Of those that *are* vulnerable, beating them requires tracking key card groups which target that specific side bet. Some blackjack pros do attack certain side bets, but an amateur trying to get lucky has no long range shot.

House edges on side bets range from about $2^1/2$% up to over 20%! Compare that against $^1/3$% to $^2/3$% for proper basic strategy blackjack. Even with just $5 on one of the better side bets at say 3% and $15 on your hand, you'll be fading 1.2% on the combined $20. That'll tend to drain you twice as fast as $20 on the hand!

If you believe your favorite side bet is a good deal, then bet the side bet and the blackjack hand from two separate chip stacks. Keep track of how each stack does over the long haul. Sooner or later, that should cure you! If you're a regular basic strategy player and never make a side bet, *your bankroll will thank you!*

For more in-depth coverage of side bets, see Arnold Snyder's *Big Book of Blackjack*, or go online to *Wizardofodds.com* or *APheat.com*, then to *blackjack side bets*.

RULE VARIATIONS

At every casino the blackjack games will look just about the same. But when it comes down to the nuts and bolts, each house has its own little set of personalized "sub rules". How many decks do they use? Can you double down after splits? How many times can you re-split a pair -- if at all? Does the dealer stand or hit on *soft 17?* What about "surrender"?

How much difference can these rules make? There *could* be as much as a 1% difference between the best games and the worst. But the vast majority will fall within a $^1/2$% of each other.

The following chart breaks things down rule by rule. It uses a *reference base/starting point* of:

Four decks	No Double after Split
Stand on Soft 17	Re-Split Pairs to 4 hands
Double on any 1st two cards	Split Aces only once
No Surrender	

With that setup, a basic strategy player has an even **0.50%** disadvantage. Add and subtract the percentages below as your rules and decks vary.

RULE	PLAYER GAIN
1 Deck *(instead of 4)*	+0.50%
2 Decks *(instead of 4)*	+0.15%
6 Decks *(instead of 4)*	-0.07%
8 Decks *(instead of 4)*	-0.10%
Dealer hits soft 17	-0.21%
No Double on 9	-0.10%
No Soft Doubling	-0.11%
No Re-Splits, normal Pairs *(1 dk.)*	-0.02%
No Re-Splits, normal Pairs *(8 dks.)*	-0.06%
No Hole Card *(double loses original)*	0.00%
No Hole Card *(double loses all)*	-0.13%
Blackjack pays 6-to-5 *(single deck)*	-1.39% (corrected)
Double After Split	+0.14%
Re-Split Aces *(1 dk.)*	+0.03%
Re-Split Aces *(8 dks.)*	+0.07%
Surrender *(1 dk, stand A/6)*	+0.02%
Surrender *(6 dks, stand A/6)*	+0.07%
Surrender *(8 dks, hit A/6)*	+0.10%
Early Surrender against 10 only	+0.24%

Using the table on the previous page, here's how you'd figure the house edge over a basic strategy player with these two rather "middle-of-the-road" blackjack setups *(examples "A" and "B" are the rules that were used in computer simulations throughout this book to determine the performance of various playing strategies).*

GAME "A"		GAME "B"	
Reference base	-0.50%	Reference base	-0.50%
Six decks	-0.07%	Two decks	+0.15%
Stands on Soft17	0.00%	Hits Soft 17	-0.21%
Double after split	+0.14%	Double after split	+0.14%
No Re-splits	-0.05%	Re-split to 4 hds.	0.00%
	-0.48%		**-0.42%**

THE DEATH OF INNOCENCE

Now you've been all the way around the block regarding basic strategy blackjack. It's a completely automatic mode of play that should be totally unaffected by anything you may think or see. Indeed, the basic strategist plays the game like a mindless *robot.*

But right on the next page is where all that begins to change. As you progress *beyond* basic strategy, it becomes both your privilege and *responsibility* to notice outside factors which will influence your decisions for the better. That's where you start to become an honest to goodness "card player" at the blackjack table.

Chapter 5
KEY POINTS

1) For the typical player, the Basic Strategy is the most efficient way to play all his hands. Using it will typically cut the house edge down to $1/2$%.

2) For novices, the "Blackjack Starter Kit" is much easier to learn at the expense of an additional $1/2$% house edge.

3) Although millions of people play blackjack, most of them misplay the same hands.

4) Not following through with your hands by failing to double after a split, not re-splitting a re-paired pair, or stopping short on a multi-card *16* can boost the house edge another $1/3$%.

5) Taking "even money" on a blackjack when the dealer has an Ace showing is the single most widespread strategic error made in the blackjack universe.

6) As a group, the most consistently misplayed hands are "soft" double downs".

7) Many experienced players still wrongly believe it's good to to insure their *"20"* when in fact, that's usually the worst possible time to take Insurance!

8) The dealer will break 17% of the time with a playable *Ace* showing and 42% of the time with a *6* up. There is no up-card with which the dealer will break more often than not.

9) Doubling down for less than the full amount is virtually always a horrible play!

10) Rule variations and numbers of decks in play can have as much as a 1% effect on the overall percentages, but most games fall within a $1/2$% window.

6

What comes after Basic Strategy?

The vast majority of avid blackjack buffs commit their basic strategy to memory, play the game as a $^1/_2$% underdog and stagnate there. Why? Because in most books, the next step beyond basic strategy is card counting. And from the comfortable plateau of basic strategy, card counting is a quantum leap up into a much more technical and demanding realm.

Most serious blackjack players just want the best chance to win that they can get without enduring the meticulous chore of tracking a shoe full of cards. If this is you, remaining a "vanilla" basic strategy player doesn't have to be the end of the line -- at least, not quite because;

THERE ARE STILL SEVERAL SKILLS YOU CAN LEARN SHORT OF CARD COUNTING, THAT WILL IMPROVE YOUR GAME BEYOND BASIC STRATEGY

Practically speaking, these refinements will *not* be enough to actually give you the upper hand in the overall game. The old axiom still remains true that you simply have to count at least *some* cards to be an out-and-out winner at blackjack. But adding the concepts from this chapter to your basic strategy play can cut

85

about $^3/_{10}$% off that last $^1/_2$% advantage the casino holds over you. That in turn, will save you money and convert a few of your playing sessions from losers into winners.

This chapter then, is dedicated to the huge multitude of players wallowing in that vast gap between basic strategy and card counting -- *who want more.*

The first fine-tuning technique described here won't come in handy very often in today's games, since it applies only to single deck play. But it's still a concept that should be understood by the "thinking" player. So let's get it spelled out right up front.

INSURANCE for BASIC STRATEGY??

Now, just what did I mean in the last chapter when I said, *"You should practically never take Insurance"*? Most blackjack books will tell you to completely ignore the Insurance proposition unless you're a card counter. Well, that's *practically* right.

However, even if you don't count cards there are still a few opportunities to make an advantageous Insurance wager in single deck games. And it has nothing to do with whether you have a good or bad hand! It only has to do with the odds against winning the Insurance bet. Take a look at the illustration below:

There's just one other player at the table and you have gotten a glimpse at his cards *(which is easy to do)!* Notice that there are no *10's* among either of your hands.

The point here is, it doesn't matter whether it's the first hand off the top of the deck, or you're thirty cards into it and haven't been paying attention to what's been played out. Either way, where you're concerned the dealer could have any one of 47 cards in the hole and 16 of them would be a *10*. That's over one-third winners for you on a bet that pays 2-to-1 odds.

So get some Insurance money out there! You now have a 2.1% edge on the Insurance wager instead of the usual 5.9% single deck disadvantage. If you could see a third hand and that player held no *10's* either, your Insurance edge would climb to 6.7%! This is how shifting odds can work in the player's favor.

Don't be concerned about the cards that may have already gone by just because you don't know what they were. They're in exactly the same category as the cards still remaining in the deck; *unknown!* Even though your information may not be as complete as you'd like, *any card you can't eliminate by having seen it must be considered available to be the dealer's hole card!*

The following chart itemizes the single deck opportunities for profitable Insurance betting by a non-counting blackjack player. Look them over. Should one of these situations pop up when you're at the table, *take Insurance!*

NO. of HANDS SEEN	MAXIMUM NO. of TENS
2	0
3	0
4	1

Look at the bottom row. If you can see four players hands including your own and there's no more than one *10* among them when the dealer's got an *Ace* up, *take Insurance.* That's because 35% of the unseen cards *(15 out of 43)* are *10's*. Other than using the information above, it's true that a basic strategy player should simply forget the Insurance proposition exists.

*The rest of the fine-tuning skills in this chapter apply to **any** number of decks. Each of them will squeeze a bit more out of your game. But first.......*

DO COMPS HAVE STRATEGIC VALUE?

Can the casino comps you get from playing blackjack amount to anything worthwhile? If you're a $10 bettor, probably not. But if you play *good* basic strategy at a $25 level or above, your comps can often cut your already small disadvantage in half, or *further*. Entire books have been devoted to strategically maximizing casino comps, but here's a more generic breakdown for mid-level players.

If you play $25 blackjack for a few hours on a player's card, the floorperson, at your request is likely to comp you a pass for a buffet or the coffee shop. Also, if you're a local regular you might be mailed some monthly $10 cash coupons *(bigger players often get free hotel rooms, shopping certificates, sporting event tickets, etc.)*

These days, a typical $25 blackjack game carries about a $^6/_{10}$% basic strategy house edge. So if you visit that casino twice a month for three hours each time and play *perfect* basic strategy, you figure to lose $75 for the month -- plus/minus a $650 *standard* luck factor. If you have totally *average* luck and cash a $10 coupon each visit, you'll still be out $55. Then, if you value those two free meals at say, $15 each, it'll cut your *combined* monthly cost to around $25. Now, that $^6/_{10}$% *gross* house edge will *net* down close to $^2/_{10}$%.

Of course, the casino doesn't typically expect to earn only $75 from your monthly play. An ordinary blackjack hack will generally dump more like $200 on your kind of action, and two meal comps probably don't cost the casino $30 anyway. So they usually won't mind comping you $50 in *perks* to coax you back in next month.

The point is, once you trim the house edge down to a little nub with basic strategy, getting a tad extra makes things a pretty darn close gamble. In the example above, if you play 72 hours for the year with no comps, Lady Luck *(one standard deviation)* will *usually* have you finishing that year in a window somewhere between +**$1300** and -**$3100**. But if you redeem that $600 in cash / food comps, your *net* window will shift to +**$1900 / -$2500**. You still won't have the overall edge in the game, but you *will* have a wider opening on the *plus* side of that slippery *luck factor* window.

87.1

2017 UPDATE

Playing Misdeals; the 'IN' or 'OUT' Option

Misdeals occur pretty seldom in blackjack, but when they do it'd be nice to know how to manage your hand in a freak situation.

Typical misdeals arise when the dealer skips a card to one of the players, or gives an unwanted hit. In these cases, the floor person often rules that since the cards are now out of order, every player can opt to either remain in the hand – or pull back his bet and get out *(the option is usually given **before** the dealer checks under any 10 or **Ace**)*. Obviously, you should play the hand if you're a favorite to win, and fold it if you're an underdog. But your chances may not be what they seem. Suppose you've got;

What's your move? Fact is, with a **4** up the dealer will make a completed hand 60% of the time, and most of those will beat **17!** You're a 7-to-6 underdog in this spot and should pull out. In fact;

---

17 is an underdog to any dealer's up-card except **6,** which is a virtual tossup.
18 is a favorite against an **8** or *lower.* **Fold** it against a **9** or *higher.*
19 is a favorite against a **9** or *lower.* **Fold** against an *unchecked* **10** or **Ace.**
20 is always a solid favorite and should be **played** against any up-card.
Any **"stiff"** *(hard 12 thru 16)* is **always** an underdog and should be **folded.**
Play with **7** or less, *only* against a **6.**
Play with **8** against a **3** thru **7.** **Play** with **9** against an **8** or *lower.*
Fold with **10** vs. an *unchecked* **10** or **Ace.** **Fold 11** vs. an *unchecked* **Ace.**
Play Ace/2 or **Ace/3** against an **8** or *lower.*
Play Ace/4 *only* against a **3** thru **7.** **Play Ace/5** *only* against a **3** thru **6.**
Play Ace/6 against a **7** or *lower.* **Play Ace/7** against an **8** or *lower.*
Play a pair of **2s** thru **7s** against a **4, 5** or **6** – *also* **play** **2/2** and **4/4** vs. a **7.**
Play 8/8 or **9/9** against any *lower* up-card. **Fold** vs. an *equal* or *higher* one.
Play A/A against any **10** or *lower.* **Fold** against an **Ace** if it's *unchecked.*

87.2

This next refinement is simple to use and will get you to play two of your hands just a tad more accurately than plain basic strategy.

COMPOSITION-SENSITIVE HANDS

A basic strategy chart means just what the word says – *basic.* It was originally developed to give you a clear, definitive, black and white way to play all your starting hands. In that regard, it's a life saver. Browsing over a basic strategy chart though, you tend to get the impression that all the correct plays are equally correct. This is not really the case. Here's what I mean.

When you have *16* against an *Ace*, odds are you'll win the hand 24 times out of 100 if you hit *(counting pushes as a half win and a half loss)*, but only 17 times if you stand. Mathematically, it's a no-brainer. You've got to hit it every single time since it's not even close. If you don't, you'll be hurting your chances to win the hand, big time! In fact, that's how it is with most hands.

A couple of hands however, are **extremely** borderline situations. These marginal hands are such close calls that;

**THE BEST POSSIBLE WAY TO PLAY THEM
ACTUALLY DEPENDS UPON WHICH SPECIFIC
CARDS WERE "KILLED" TO MAKE UP THE HAND**

That's why they're called "composition-sensitive" – they fall into a *grey area*. Ahh, but the basic strategy doesn't deal in grey areas! It deals in black and white! So when a composition-sensitive hand comes up, the basic strategy just tells you to always play it the one way which would be best overall – even though that's not *always* best. Look at the hand below.

Now, with *this* hand you should win 23½ times out of 100 if you hit it *(counting pushes as a half win and a half loss)*. And what if you stand? Then you only win 23 out of 100. *Surprised at how close it is?* The basic strategy simply says to hit here because even though it's very close, you indeed do just a smidge better by hitting *10/6* against a *10* than by standing. **There is however, a tiny problem with this!**

The problem is that this is only a *"starting"* 16. Notice that all three cards which were killed *(removed from play)* to make up this exact hand would bust you if they were still available as "hit" cards. However, they are *not* available, and with such a marginal hand that's a contributing factor as to why you should hit.

But then, what about all those times you're dealt *12* against a *10* up, hit and catch a *4* to make *16?* Or maybe you start out with *6/3*, then hook a *5* followed by a *deuce.* How about *4/4/4/4* against that *picture card* showing? If the situation was so close before, should you still hit now? In the majority of cases, the answer is *NO!* But the basic strategy does not take the trouble to differentiate between "multi-card" holdings and "two-card" starting hands! This is what composition-sensitive hands are all about.

The "Rule of 45": The *10/6* shown in the previous illustration is your most classic version of *16.* However, roughly half of all the times you have *16,* it'll be the "built up" variety. And counting all its forms, you'll find yourself in the annoying situation of having *16* against a *10* roughly one hand out of every thirty over the rest of your blackjack days. That's about once every twenty minutes!

It was mentioned earlier in Chapter **5** that if you hit *16* against a *10* and are lucky enough to stay alive by catching something like a *2,* you're still probably going to lose the hand. This is quite true. What you're really looking to catch here is a *4* or a *5. But if your 16 contains any 4's or 5's in it, you've killed one or two of your own key cards!* In that case, you actually have a smidge better chance to win by standing rather than hitting! Yep, it's true! The bottom line of it all is;

AGAINST A *10* UP, IF YOUR *16* CONTAINS ANY *4's* or *5's* -- STAND!

That's the *"Rule of 45"*. It breaks the basic strategy down into finer detail. You should do this even with eight decks, although the fewer the decks, the more difference it makes. A *classic* stand situation would be a *16* made up of *7/5/4* since it contains **both** a *4* and a *5!* You don't **need** to have both though. You should also stand against a *10* with hands like *9/5/2* or *4/3/9* -- anything that contains a *4* or a *5*. But if you've built something like an *A/6/8/A,* you should still hit because you haven't drawn any cards out of play that would have done much for your hand. Here are two vivid pictures to illustrate the *Rule of 45* in action:

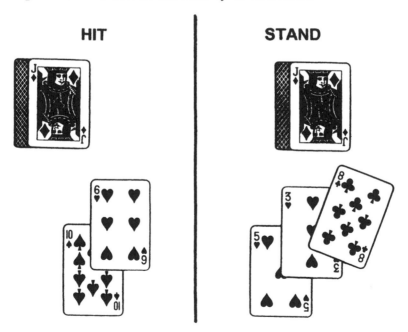

| HIT | STAND |

CAUTION: Now don't become overzealous and start standing with the likes of *7/5/4* against other high up-cards. ***The "Rule of 45" applies only to a dealer's 10 up.*** Against other high up-cards, you're not drawing as slim to win it.

90

The "Doctor Pepper Rule":

Your second composition-sensitive hand arises when you have *12* against a *4* up. When the basic strategy flatly states that you should stand with this hand, it doesn't tell you what a hairline close decision it is. But actually, the exact cards which make up your *12*, the number of decks in use and what the dealer does on *soft 17* determine your best play.

So if the game is a multi-deck shoe which **ALSO** *hits on soft 17*, then just stand with **any** *12* against a *4*. But with one or two decks – **OR** – in any *stand on soft 17* game, follow the Doctor Pepper Rule. It's a tad sharper way to play this hand than vanilla basic strategy. ***The key is whether your 12 contains a 10 or not.***

When you've got *10/2* specifically, against a *4* that's a Doctor Pepper hand. If you hit it, there's one less *10* available to bust you.

Now let's switch it and give you a *7/5*. That puts the busting *10* back in the shoe, while it kills two chances for you to make *17* or *19*! If you held an *8/4* or *9/3*, you'd have one less chance to make *20* or *21*, with the extra *10* still lurking! These flip-flops set *10/2* apart from the other *12s* in this spot! In fact, it's correct to **hit** *10/2* against a *4* in any *stand on soft 17* game – **OR** – with two or fewer decks regardless of the *soft 17* rule! See the picture below:

STAND	HIT

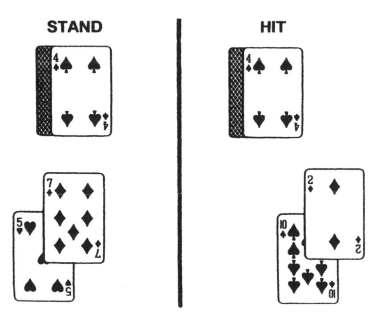

To recap; in shoe games that *hit soft 17*, **stand** on **all** *12s* against a *4*. But with one or two decks, or in *any stand on soft 17* game;

HIT *10/2* AGAINST A *4* UP, BUT STAND
WITH ANY OTHER KIND OF HARD *12*

Again, don't get carried away and start hitting *10/2* against a *5* or a *6*. Those hands are not that close a decision. ***The Dr. Pepper Rule means "10-2-4" exclusively!***

Beware that when you change up your play and make these two composition-sensitive adjustments, you'll often get degrading criticisms from the know-it-alls at your table. Don't explain your reasons to them. As far as they're concerned, you're an idiot and you're not going to change their minds. Just let things go at that.

Now if you think *those* two "renegade" plays will draw static from other players at the table, then this next, more advanced refinement ought to really set them off.

---

*If noticing the specific cards that compose your hand can help you play a couple of them more effectively, then what about all the other cards on board? Well, if you use that information properly, then you'll be able to adjust your play -- not with **two** hands -- but with **seven**! That's more thorough than simple hand composition because it takes more information into account.*

The "MAGNIFICENT 7"
BLACKJACK HANDS

Up to this chapter in the book, you've been a "rote" blackjack player obediently hitting and standing without really understanding why. But from this point on, blackjack starts to become a legitimate game of skill beyond the scope of just memorizing a chart or two. In order to play *beyond* basic strategy effectively, you're going to have to become a bit of a *"card player"* in your own right. You'll need to understand why you hit, stand or double when you do. And through that understanding you'll learn to *"tweak"* your play with a number of hands in the right spots.

What are *"the Magnificent 7 Blackjack Hands"*? Well, you've just seen how the cards that compose certain holdings can affect how you should play them — yet plain basic strategy only considers the dealer's up-card and your hand *total*. Yes, *Composition-Sensitive* play breaks it down one tiny step further by measuring the effects of card variations within that total. But the *Magnificent 7 Hands* go one step beyond that;

BY FACTORING IN ALL THE CARDS ON THE BOARD

Using this *extra* information, you can make playing decisions that are slightly superior to basic strategy with seven different hands. They're listed below.

the Magnificent 7 Hands

9 vs. a **2** up
12 vs. a **4** up
13 vs. a **2** up
16 vs. a **10** up
A/2 vs. a **5** up
A/4 vs. a **4** up
A/8 vs. a **6** up

The basic strategy plays for these hands are correct by only a narrow margin. And that's if everything's *exactly normal!* But many times you'll be in a position to notice that everything is *not* exactly normal. About once every eighteen hands, you'll be dealt one of the seven hands above. That's when you should take a look around the board. In a shoe game there'll often be a dozen or more face-up cards to be seen in the hands of the other players. And with the *Magnificent 7* hands, seeing a dozen cards is more useful than seeing just three.

Babies vs. 10s: Here's how to tell when you should change
up your play with these seven hands. Blackjack is basically just a game of high and low cards. The *10*-counters are the high cards. The low cards are all the *2s, 3s, 4s* and *5s*. We'll call those low cards, *"Babies"*. So in any full number of decks there are just as many *Babies* as *10s*. A complete six deck shoe for example would

93

contain 96 *Babies* and 96 *Tens.* It turns out that with the *Magnificent 7 Hands,* if just a few extra *10s* or a few extra *Babies* have come out;

THE BASIC STRATEGY IS NO LONGER
THE BEST WAY TO PLAY

So when you scan the board *(including your own hand and the dealer's up-card)* while holding one of these hands, compare the number of exposed *Babies* to *10s.* Which are there more of? This will tell you how to play those seven hands more accurately than plain basic strategy.

The table which follows has been calibrated to the six deck shoe -- which has become somewhat of a standard for modern day blackjack. If the right cards have come out on the board, you should make the following adjusted plays. *(Board counts for double deck will follow after a thorough six deck explanation).*

"MAGNIFICENT 7" QUALIFICATIONS
FOR THE SIX DECK SHOE

HAND	IF BOARD HAS	ADVANCED PLAY
9 vs. 2	*five* more Babies than 10s *(min.)*	DOUBLE
12 vs. 4	*any* more 10s than Babies	HIT
13 vs. 2	*five* more 10s than Babies *(min.)*	HIT
16 vs. 10	*any* more Babies than 10s	STAND
A/2 vs. 5	*any* more 10s than Babies	just HIT
A/4 vs. 4	*any* more 10s than Babies	just HIT
A/8 vs. 6	*four* more Babies than 10s *(min.)*	DOUBLE

If your board count doesn't meet the above requirements, then just follow the basic strategy. The picture on the next page shows a situational opportunity with a *Magnificent 7* hand.

Suppose you're halfway through a six deck shoe and have no idea what's been played thus far. You're sitting at third base. There are three other players at the table and they all have *20*. *In this situation you're actually better off hitting your 13 against a deuce!*

94

When the basic strategy says to stand with this hand, it assumes you have 94 *Babies* and 95 *Tens* to draw from. Using that information, yes, you should stand. But in the example shown, as far as you can tell you still have 94 *Babies*, but only 89 *Tens (a net shortage of five available 10's)*. Standing was the correct play for *some other* deck composition -- but for *this* composition, the best play is to *hit!* Here's another slightly advanced play:

This time you're sitting in center field with a *soft 19* against the dealer's *6*. With the five net excess *Babies* on this board, **your percentage play is now to double down!** The dealer is more likely than usual to have *16* and you're a little more likely to make another *19* with your next hit. You've got to do it! Yeah, you'll get plenty of stares from all the "experts" at your table. That comes with the territory. But you're playing the game at a deeper level than they realize exists.

Now let me call your attention to a potentially confusing fact about board counting the *Babies* vs. *10's*:

PLAYING THE MAGNIFICENT 7 HANDS CORRECTLY WILL SUPERSEDE NOT ONLY BASIC STRATEGY, BUT ALSO COMPOSITION-SENSITIVE STRATEGY

That's because the other cards on the board can contain enough extra *Babies* or *10's* to counteract those in your hand. Here's what I mean:

There you are at third base with everybody's favorite hand, *16* against a *10*. *Basic strategy* says to hit. *Composition-sensitive* strategy says to hit. But the *Magnificent 7* strategy says to stand! **That's because the basic strategy and the composition-sensitive strategy don't know that all those other Babies are dead.** The most complete information you have tells you that in this particular spot, you're better off standing!

THIS IS TRUE EVEN THOUGH YOU
HAVE *10/6* RATHER THAN SAY, *7/5/4*

When you have a *Magnificent 7* hand, your board count outranks the other two strategies. You see, it's the **total** of *10s* vs. *Babies* that matters more than just what's in your own hand. You can get this prioritized in your mind by visualizing the following list:

HIERARCHY of PLAY

#3) BASIC STRATEGY *overridden by*
#2) HAND COMPOSITION *overridden by*
#1) BOARD CONDITION

The basic strategy is your most *elementary* level of hand analysis. Hand composition is *a little more exact* than that. And counting up all the *Babies* vs. *10s* on board is *more comprehensive yet.* It simply knows more. These next two hands illustrate that point.

Close Call Soft Doubles: These arise whenever you're dealt

A/2 vs. *5*   or   *A/4* vs. *4*

Most players will double with either of these hands in a heartbeat. But doubling here is just ever-so-slightly better than hitting – *usually.* Now, notice that holding either hand by itself puts two more *Babies* on board than *10s*. But – if the **entire** combined board should happen to contain even one more **net 10** than *Babies*;

YOU SHOULD NOT DOUBLE EITHER HAND!

Those three extra dead *10s* have just shaded the dealer's bust chances down to where you should now simply take a hit.

Dead Cards in the Discard Tray: As you're digesting all this, you might wonder to yourself, *"Yeah, but if I see a bunch of 10s on board, how can it be right to adjust my play without knowing how many offsetting Babies may have come out earlier?"* The answer is, if 150 cards have been dealt thus far it would indeed be best if you knew all 150 *(as with card counting).* Then you could make some very informed decisions with many more hands. Still – being able to eliminate eight or ten cards from contention is more helpful than eliminating only three. In effect, it's a freeze-frame tiny snippet of card counting. Every card you can see at the time is unavailable to come out of the shoe. As for the dead cards in the discard tray? All unknown cards must be considered still live.

This is proper logic since it doesn't matter that there are 150 cards already played out if you have no idea what they were. That puts them in the exact same category with those still in the shoe – *theoretically available**. You're simply reacting as accurately as possible to the information you've gleaned from all the cards on the board, and that's enough to improve your playing efficiency with this rather borderline hand.

*theoretically available – the thing to understand is that in reality, none of the cards behind the very next one in the shoe can come out next either. But since their identity is unknown they, along with all the discards are as far as you know, eligible.

"MAGNIFICENT 7" QUALIFICATIONS
FOR DOUBLE DECK PLAY

When you see a bunch of cards spread out on the board, the fewer decks you're playing with, the greater effect those cards will have. For this reason, you don't need nearly the imbalance to trigger an adjusted play in hand held games that you need with the shoe. The trouble is though, you won't *see* as many cards either because most double deck games are dealt face-down. Counting the other players' hit cards, busts and maybe the hole cards on your left and/or right, you might catch 4 or 5 cards.

As of late though, a few casinos are beginning to deal their double deck games face-up. This would be a good spot for basic strategy players, enabling them to correctly change up their play quite often due to unbalanced board layouts.

HAND	IF BOARD IS	ADVANCED PLAY
9 vs. 2	*less* than 2 extra Babies	just HIT
12 vs. 4	*even* or has more Tens	HIT
13 vs. 2	*plus* 2 Tens	HIT
16 vs. 10	*plus* 1 Baby	STAND
A/2 vs. 5	*plus* 1 Ten	just HIT
A/4 vs. 4	*plus* 1 Ten	just HIT
A/8 vs. 6	*plus* 2 Tens	STAND

98

Playing all the "Mag 7" hands with an eight deck shoe isn't going to be worth your trouble. You'll need to see too many excess *Babies* or *10s* to pull the trigger. Just stand with *16* against a *10* whenever there are more *Babies* on board than *10s* and be done with it.

So how much can playing the *Mag 7* hands according to the exposed board cards help your overall game over straight basic strategy? Well, 2.5 billion computer simulated blackjack hands indicate it should reduce the house edge by about the following:

SINGLE DECK	**.07%**
DOUBLE DECK	**.03%**
SIX DECK	**.02%**

It's disappointingly little, I know. A $25 bettor might save 50 cents an hour using this information. But realize that any one basic strategy hand play also saves you only a very small amount – but there are 340 different hands! For example, a $25 bettor also saves about 50 cents/hour by hitting all *soft 18s* against a *10*.

It may simplify things to know that the main chunk of your *Mag 7* help comes from just varying your play with *16* against a *10* and with *12* against a *4*. It's pretty easy to recognize when those two hands should be "tweaked". The upcoming strategy *mini-card* should help with that, plus some other testy problems.

2017 UPDATE

TROUBLE BLACKJACK HANDS & BOARD TWEAKS

By this point in the book you should already know about 90% of your correct basic strategy. Keeping a full basic strategy chart on your person would just be redundant overkill. All you need now is something to remind you how to play those tricky hands – the ones that most players still miss. You'll also want to know which hands to change up when the dealer hits *soft 17*.

That's what the card on the following page is for. It contains only a fraction of the hands that a basic strategy card has, and is the size of a credit card. The card also points out your *hit soft 17* strategy changes. Lastly, it tells you when to "tweak" the two most common board-sensitive hands based on *Babies vs. 10s* on board.

Blackjack Trouble Hands
4 to 8 decks w/ double after split

LOW DEALER'S UP-CARD

your hand	2	3	4	5	6
9					
12			+T	STAND	
A/2; A/3	HIT				
A/4; A/5				DOUBLE	
A/6					
A/7					
A/8					D
2/2;3/3;7/7					
4/4					
6/6		SPLIT			
9/9					

HIGH DEALER'S UP-CARD

your hand	7	8	9	10	A
2/2;3/3;7/7					
9/9					
A/7					
10					
11					D
16			+B		

This card contains only those hands that still might be giving you trouble. Although it's small, its fewer hand cells are large enough to be easily read in a casino environment.

PAIR SPLITS: Note that the pair splits shown are for games in which you *can* double after splitting *(DAS),* since this is normally the prevailing rule in shoe games.

HITS SOFT 17: The two boxes with a bold "*D*" in them tell you that if the dealer hits *soft 17,* you should double down with *11* against an *Ace* and also with *Ace/8* against a *6.*

BOARD-SENSITIVE HANDS: Finally, the "+*T*" in the box for *12* against a *4* states that if there are more *Tens* on board than *Babies, you should hit that 12!* Likewise, the "+*B*" in the *16* vs. *10* box instructs you to *stand with 16* if there are more *Babies* on board than *Tens!* Always include your own hand and the dealer's up-card along with the other board cards in your tally. Ahh, but what if there happens to be the same total number of *Babies* as *Tens?*

THEN JUST PLAY BASIC STRATEGY

Deviate from basic *only* when there are *more Tens* with *12* against a *4* -- and *more Babies* with *16* against a *10*. These are the opposite of what you will usually find to be the case.

GET OVER IT: Now, don't feel as though you're committing heresy when you "break" basic strategy in qualifying situations. Remember that these are "borderline" hands. When basic strategy has determined that you should just barely hit *10/6* against a *10*, but the other cards on board are *3-4-5-8*, basic strategy has assumed that *3-4-5-8* was still available! If basic strategy were calculated with a *3-4-5-8* gone:

IT WOULD TELL YOU TO "WAVE" YOUR *10/6*

Remember, you're at a point in your game where you're trying to notice and take advantage of things that go beyond "zero memory" basic strategy! You're starting to become a blackjack "card player", not a basic strategy robot.

Copy and keep this card with you until you know this stuff cold. All it will do right now is take the level of your game just a hair above basic strategy. But it'll teach you to begin noticing things you'll need to in order to become a true winning player later.

This next facet of the game has scarcely, if ever been touched upon in any other blackjack book. Yet, every serious player should have knowledge of it. Opportunities to use, and profit from this technique will come up several times virtually every day you play. What you need to have is the blackjack "card sense" to take advantage of something called:

HAND INTERACTION

Filling in Doubles: Suppose the player next to you has the classic *11* against a dealer's *face-card* with a $20 bet up. He pauses, tinkers with his chips, thinks some more and finally shoves out just two more red chips, doubling for *less*. This is not an unusual play -- a poor one, but not all that unusual. Apparently, his fear of that old fable, *"The dealer always has a 10 in the hole"* has warped his judgment. Actually, the player is a 6-to-5 favorite to win here, even when being limited to one hit. That's a 9% edge! So what can you do about it?

TOSS YOUR OWN $10 OVER THERE AND SAY, "I'LL GO WITH YOU ON THIS ONE, PARTNER."

When are you ever going to have a known 9% edge on your own hand before you even put a bet down? Well here, that's exactly what you have. If this player doesn't know enough to take the whole advantage to himself, *you take the rest!* This is just one of the many *hand interaction* plays that can improve your overall expectation at the table. Hand interaction plays come in several forms. They're listed below:

1) Taking part or all of another player's profitable double.
2) Giving away part of your own *unprofitable* split.
3) Taking part of another player's profitable split.
4) Buying or partnering on another's advantageous hand.
5) Making profitable side-bets with other players.

With regard to #1, you should always offer to fill in another player's double whenever he makes a correct double down for less than the maximum. That should be obvious. But what's not so obvious is that *you can also gain an edge by taking part of another player's **incorrect** double down!* Look at the picture below:

You're at third base. *Your* hand doesn't matter, but the player on your right has *9* against a *7*. Now, maybe he thinks doubling here is a good play or maybe he's just been running "good". But either way, he decides to gamble and doubles for less than the max.

Now, *9* against a dealer's *7* is a bad double -- *but do you know why?* It's because doubling will win 53% of the time, where just hitting will win 59% *(counting pushes as a half win and a half loss)*. Both hitting *and* doubling will make money, but hitting makes *more* money. That's why he should just hit it. However, *his* mistake is *your* opportunity.

You see, as the person holding the hand, his options were 59% or 53%. But now, your options as a bystander are to jump in on a 53% shot -- or do nothing. And a 53% shot still carries a 6% edge. *So get your money over there!* You can't get a 6% edge by watching other people play their winning hands.

The point is that even though a player may violate basic strategy with a bad double down, many of them still carry a net edge, albeit a reduced edge at that. So if it's done for less than the maximum, you should complete his double with your own money. The following chart lists those double downs which are normally incorrect *(in multi-deck play)* for the player holding the hand -- yet would still provide a net edge to a bystander who partakes in them.

8 vs. a **5** up	**A/3** vs. a **4** up
8 vs. a **6** up	**A/7** vs. a **2** up
9 vs. a **2** up	**A/8** vs. a **3** up
9 vs. a **7** up	**A/8** vs. a **4** up
11 vs. an **A** up	**A/8** vs. a **5** up
A/2 vs. a **4** up	**A/8** vs. a **6** up

Some of your edges will be very small here, such as with *8* against a *5*. There, you'll win your bet just a hair over half the time. Yet with other hands such as *Ace/8* against a *6*, you'll win better than 60% of your bets *(again, after adjusting for pushes)*. Your bread and butter play though, *(because it will come up more often and because many players make it)* will be *11* against an *Ace*. There, your edge will average about 7% of whatever you put up.

101

Also, many times a player many be thinking of doubling, but won't be quite sure. If it's on a hand where he'll obviously take only one hit regardless of what card he catches, you can offer to make the entire double in place of his doing it at all. A good example would be with something like *A/6* against a *4.* He's going to take a card anyway and he'll never want a second hit. His worst possible hit card would be a *5* giving him *12* -- with which he'd stand anyway.

I *do not* however, recommend making the entire double for somebody on a hand like *8* against a *5* or *6* up. If he catches a *2* or a *3* here, he'll be stuck with *10* or *11* and repercussions could develop at the table when he can't hit it again. If you're going to make the entire double on another player's hand, choose something that's a "one hit only" hand.

Pawning Splits: Another profitable phase of hand interaction involves pair splitting. These get pretty tricky. Look at the next illustration:

Again, you're at third base. The other player probably knows he's supposed to split a pair of *7's* against a *deuce*, but for some reason he just doesn't feel like gambling the extra money. So, looking for a cheap way to get out of his *14,* he asks you if you want to put up

102

the extra bet and play one of his *7's* while he takes the other. Opportunities like this come up all the time. Should you take it?

The answer is -- ***not in this situation!*** Why? Because if you did, you'd have only a 46% chance to win your bet *(after adjusting for pushes).* That's a losing venture! Then why is it correct basic strategy to split two *7's* against a *deuce* in the first place, you ask? Because if you don't, your *14* will win only 35% of the time *(when the dealer breaks).* And winning two hands 46% of the time each, loses less money than winning one hand 35% of the time.

This particular split, like so many others is a "defensive" pair split because you split to *reduce your loss.* But if you're only a bystander, *you have no loss to reduce* -- so just sit this one out!

Then how can you benefit from interacting on pair splits? Well, here's where hand interaction can get ethically sensitive. Fundamentally, blackjack is a game played strictly against the house. Most casual players aren't expecting to be *snookered* by somebody else at the table. Out of basic respect, casual players should probably be left to their solitary game. But other diehards, particularly at higher limits are looking for any kind of edge, and often barter with each other using their own judgment.

So when you're at a table with these more entrepreneurial types, if ***you have*** those two *7's* against a *deuce (or several other pairs like it),* you might say;

"I DON'T LIKE THIS HAND, BUT I'M GONNA SPLIT IT ANYWAY -- DOES ANYBODY WANT HALF?"

Since it looks like a decent hand, but isn't, you might get rid of half of an underdog pair. Then, you'll get to play *7* against a *deuce* one time only, rather than twice.

The list below contains strictly "defensive" pair splits. You'll save *further* money beyond basic strategy with all these if you should pawn one of their pair cards off to another player.

2/2 vs. a **2** or **3**	**7/7** vs. a **2, 3** or **7**
3/3 vs. a **2, 3** or **7**	**8/8** vs. an **8** thru **Ace**
6/6 vs. a **2** or **3**	**9/9** vs. a **9**

Now, don't expect the guy next to you to jump up and take one of your *8's* against the dealer's *face-card.* Nobody's going to bail you half way out of that one! But two *7's* against a *2* -- or a pair of *6's*

103

against a *3?* Plenty "pseudo-experts" will like the looks of those. Just be ready to barter with these liabilities when you have them.

Buying into Splits: Now what if instead of *7/7* against a *2*, that player next to you had:

He started with a pair of *7's* against a *6*. Splitting them, he caught a *3* on his first *7*, then doubled down buying an ugly *deuce*. On his other *7* he caught a third *7* and now seems hesitant to stick yet a fourth bet out there. Since *7* against a *6* is an outright moneymaker, *you should quickly toss a bet over there and offer to absorb the cost of splitting that third 7!* When "double after splits" is allowed, you'll have a solid 10% edge on the hand. Even if "das" were not allowed, you'd still be a 3% favorite.

The list below itemizes those pair splits that will win more often than they'll lose, regardless of whether you can "das" or not. It'll always be to your advantage to get a piece of these splits whenever somebody else has the hand, *even though a few are not proper basic strategy splits.*

2/2 vs. a **5** or **6** up
3/3 vs. a **5** or **6** up
7/7 vs. a **6** up
8/8 vs. a **3** thru **7** up
9/9 vs. a **2** thru **8** up (including **7**)
10/10 vs. **anything**
A/A vs. **anything**

Hand Purchases: Still another hand interaction technique involves *buying* other players' hands which are a favorite to win. *These need to involve a wager of at least $25, and in one particular case no less than $50*, since you'll generally have to pay a premium to entice somebody to sell his hand.

One common opportunity of this type is when a player has *blackjack* against the dealer's *Ace* showing. Now nine out of ten players will take even money in this situation and that's a horrible play. But once again, this mistake leaves room for a profitable move by you. If the wager is large enough, *it would actually be to your advantage to offer that player a tiny bonus to sell you his blackjack!* Here's how it's done.

Suppose the player holding blackjack has a $50 bet on his hand and the dealer's got an *Ace* up. The dealer will immediately offer that player a flat $50 even money payoff before checking her hole card for a *10* underneath. You'll have to act quickly here by blurting out something like;

"AW, I DON'T THINK SHE HAS IT THIS TIME.
HERE, I'LL GIVE YOU EVEN MONEY, PLUS
A DOLLAR FOR YOUR HAND"

while tossing him $101 in chips. You may need to explain to the player that if he accepts this, his original $50 bet becomes yours and he's out of the hand with a $51 net win, guaranteed. *That's more than what the dealer was offering.*

As for you, you'll either get back $125 *(when the dealer doesn't have blackjack)*, or you'll just get to keep the player's original $50 bet *(when the 10 is underneath)*. But nine times out of

105

thirteen, you'll collect the $125 for a $24 profit, and the other four times you'll lose 51 bucks, net. Overall, you'll have just under a 2% edge on the $51 you were risking. If that doesn't sound like enough to bother with, where else can you earn an average of $1 in about four seconds time?

Just keep in mind that you can offer a $1 bonus for each $50 of the bet, and you'll have a 2% edge on the deal. Since most players are happy to accept even money from the dealer for their blackjacks, many will agree to accept *better* than even money from you.

One word of caution however on buying other players blackjacks: In doing this, you're actually "horning in" on the houses' action. That is, you're stopping the casino from making money on that player's mistake. For this reason, you shouldn't make this move while a floorperson is watching or if the dealer seems to be the conscientious "company type". If you do, it may be flat out disallowed or you might garner unfavorable attention.

There are also several other advantageous "hand exchange deals" you can make at the blackjack table which don't affect the house one way or the other. These are usually viewed more passively by casino personnel. *All those described on these next few pages can be made on wagers as small as $25.* Here's the first one:

Since most blackjack players tend to give the dealer credit for having a *10* in the hole, the person holding this hand will usually half expect to lose -- especially if he's been running bad. The fact however is, that a made *19* against a *playable 10* up is an 8-to-7 favorite to win! That's right; *once the dealer checks her hole card and does not have the Ace underneath, 19 will beat her more often than not.*

So if that player starts to mumble something about, *"Here goes another loser",* or appears worried about his hand, speak up! Quickly toss him $26 total for his $25 bet while saying something like;

"HERE, I'M RUNNING PRETTY GOOD, SO I'LL BUY YOUR BET FOR 26 BUCKS AND GAMBLE WITH YOUR 19"

Once again, with this arrangement the wager in the betting circle becomes yours -- this time to either double or lose. You're offering the player a guaranteed $1 profit on his *19* in the face of an impending dealer's *20* – and some will take it! After tallying up the times you win, the times you lose and the times you push, you'll average a 3% profit on each $26 invested. *(If the player's bet was $100, paying a nice round $105 would still yield a 2% advantage).* Now look at the next hand:

Most players expect to break about even with *18* against an *8,*

figuring that on average they'll push. *Wrong!* The player is a 6-to-5 favorite to win! So if somebody has this hand for $25, announce;

**"I LIKE YOUR 18 AGAINST HER 8 UP THERE.
I'LL GIVE YOU $26 FOR YOUR HAND."**

That purchase will earn you an averaged 6% on your money *(paying $105 for a $100 hand would net just under 5%)*.

Partnerships:
Players often tend to be possessive about selling off a hand that the "gambling gods" have dealt them. For this reason, simply going "halves" with somebody is often easier than buying his hand outright – and it can be done with *any size* bet.

Suppose the guy next to you has that *19* against a *10* from the picture on page 106. Like most players, he half expects to wind up looking at a *20*. So you can ease his apprehension by saying;

**"I THINK THAT 19's A WINNER;
HERE, I'LL GO HALVES WITH YOU."**

Then toss him half his bet. Clarify that a push would be "no deal". But if he wins the hand, you get your money back -- plus half the dealer's payoff. If he loses, he keeps your chips. He gets to "hedge" his *19* against a scary looking *10*, while you've just made a bet for even money that's an 8-to-7 favorite to win. You've got a 7% edge!

There are two other very common hands that are overall winners at blackjack, *but don't look like it to most players*. They are;

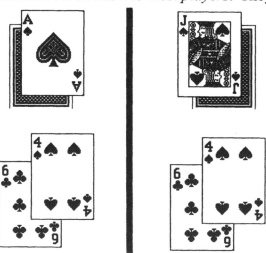

Let's say the player next to you has a starting hand of *10* when the dealer's got a *10* or *Ace* up. The dealer checks her hole card – no blackjack. Once past that hurdle, the player's *10* is favored over both a dealer's *10* or *Ace,* providing he simply plays the hand right. So if he's a competent basic strategy player, say something like;

"I'M NOT SCARED OF THAT ACE; I'LL TAKE HALF YOUR ACTION."

.....while sliding him half his bet. Do this quickly, before he starts taking hits to his hand. Be sure to explain that a push is "no bet". If like many players, he feels negative about playing an unmade hand against a fearsome *10* or *Ace,* he may be comforted by your vote of confidence and take you up on your offer.

"No-Bust" Side-Bets: When the dealer's got a *4, 5* or *6* up, the average player expects her to bust most of the time. That's why they call 'em "bust cards". This of course is a misnomer, since the dealer breaks only 40% to 42% of the time with those three up-cards. So the next time the dealer shows one of these up-cards, you can say to the player next to you:

"SHE'S DUE TO MAKE A HAND THIS TIME; I'M LAYING 6-to-5 SHE DOESN'T BUST"

Then toss either $6—or $30—or $60 towards him. Make it a comfortable amount, something less than his own bet. If he takes the odds, you'll have a 5% edge on a *5* or *6* up, and a 10% edge vs. the *4.*

The following three charts summarize all interactive hand purchases, partnerships and side-bets described in this section.

ANOTHER'S HAND	PURCHASE PRICE	YOUR EDGE
Blackjack vs. an Ace	$101 for $50	2%
19 against a 10	$26 for $25	3%
18 against an 8	$26 for $25	6%

ANOTHER'S HAND	PARTNERSHIP EDGE
19 against a 10	7%
18 against an 8	10%
10 against a 10	3%
10 against an Ace	8%

DEALER'S UP-CARD	EDGE LAYING 6-to-5
4	10%
5	5%
6	5%

109

Now, how much can all this wheeling and dealing with other players at the table help your chances to win? It depends upon how often you can get in a hand interaction play, and for how much money relative to your own bets. Getting in one extra double down every half hour for the same amount as your own bets will save you about 0.15% overall. But you shouldn't be afraid to step up your action here. If you're wagering say, $15 per hand while the guy next to you is betting $50 at a crack;

INTERACTING WITH HIS HANDS EVERY HALF HOUR CAN COMPLETELY WIPE OUT YOUR ^{1}/2% BASIC STRATEGY DISADVANTAGE!

If you're a hand interaction player, *you want bigger bettors than yourself at the table!* You'd also like your table to be as *crowded as possible* -- which does two things for you. First, the game slows down to *dilute your hourly cost* of playing basic strategy. Second, more players means *more interaction potential!* Five other players at your table will be dealt a combined 30 double downs per hour.

So if basic strategy is as far as you're going to go in blackjack, then **make this a key part of your game.** Although quite a stretch, it's technically possible to gain an overall edge in blackjack by merely combining lots of hand interaction with basic strategy.

---

*It's entirely feasible for astute recreational blackjack players to uncover a shoe in which the odds of the game have reversed and now favor the players. How can Joe Blow find such a shoe? Should he seek out "hot" tables?? Find a busting dealer?? Look for lots of blackjacks being dealt?? **Get real!** It all has to do with.........*

HIGH CARD / LOW CARD LAYOUTS

Here's a unique blackjack fact; Your odds to win at *"21"* keep changing with every card that's dealt. The overall odds of the game end up very close to 50-50, but just before the first hand of a fresh shoe, they're always 101-to-100* against you. From there they go up or down depending upon which cards have been dealt. If you keep your eyes open and know what to look for, it's

---

*Your raw odds to win the first hand outright are actually 48-to-43 against. But the possibility of a 3-to-2 blackjack payoff combined with net gains from double downs and splits flatten your "effective" odds out to 101-to-100 against.

easy to recognize when those odds have turned in your direction. How often have you noticed somebody camping behind your table, scouting the action? What's he hoping to find? He's looking for a "ripe" table. Typical gamblers believe a table is ripe when the players are getting *20's* and *blackjacks* -- or the dealer keeps busting -- or some other total nonsense. But that's not how it works. In fact, many blackjack table "scouts" jump into the action when they should run, and run when they should jump in. Why is that? Look at the following picture:

Things went pretty well for the players here. A couple of consecutive rounds like this and that "scout" behind you is likely to belly right up to the table while the gettin's good. *But he's got it all wrong!* What he saw *was* a good thing. Everybody got high cards and high cards are good for the players. But every high card that comes out when you're not there is one less high card you can get from that point on.

IF YOU'RE SCOUTING A TABLE, HIGH CARD LAYOUTS ARE A BAD THING!

If you take the ten cards from the previous picture out of a six deck shoe, what started out as a ½% basic strategy house edge now rises to 1.2%! So when you see high cards all over the place,

111

just move on down the line. Playing here would be even more likely to cost you money than if you'd picked your table blind. *What you really want is the opposite condition!*

I think it's ironic that players will often get up and leave the table just when an advantageous shoe presents itself. Now why in the world would they do that? Here's a prime example:

How do you feel when this revolting situation develops at your table? Every player had a fair to excellent start, busted off -- and then the dealer ripped off a five card *21*. Pretty disheartening isn't it? This is the point where typical players might jump up and storm off in disgust. Ahh, but they shouldn't!

At times like these, Joe Average will tend to feel that the dealer's "hot" -- or the cards are cold -- or the shoe is stacked in favor of the house. *But it's most likely not!* All that's happened here is that many of the cards which tend to help the dealer and hurt the players *(small cards)* have come out. As a rule, a barrage of small cards will kill you, just as they did in the previous illustration. But there are only so many small cards in the shoe. And when their supply diminishes, the big ones start coming out -- *and big cards help the players!* That's why;

**THE LAST THING YOU SHOULD DO WHEN YOU
SEE A LOW CARD LAYOUT IS LEAVE THE TABLE**

In fact, in this last picture the players have accrued a $1/2\%$ *advantage* on the next blind hand coming up rather than the usual $1/2\%$ *disadvantage*. If you're already there, stay and increase your bets. If you're scouting this table from behind, *get in there and gamble!*

Whether you're winning or losing has nothing to do with it. When the shoe *(or deck)* contains extra high cards, there are going to be more bonus-paying *blackjacks*, more *10's* on your double downs and the dealer will have a tougher time filling in her mandatory draws. This is the edge you came to find. *Low card layouts are your queue to move in!*

Just how low of a layout do you need? With six decks in play, if the board contains *eight* more babies than *10's*, you'll have a $1/4\%$ edge on that shoe. Anything less isn't worth risking extra money on. Here's a picture of what a "+8 baby" layout looks like:

This board has ten *babies*, only two *10's* and four "others" *(the "others" don't matter in your board analysis)*. It typifies the minimum "baby blitz" you'll be looking for. The following chart will give you insight as to how your disadvantage evaporates as more *babies* are played out of a six deck shoe.

6 Deck Shoe

Board is	Player has a
even	$1/2$% disadvantage
+6 babies	dead even game
+8 babies	$1/4$% edge
+11 babies	$1/2$% edge

Now if you're playing an eight deck shoe, it'll be pretty tough to find a low enough card layout to give you an outright edge. You'll need a "+12 baby" board just to have a $1/4$% advantage.

On the other hand, in double deck games it's easy to pin down an edge. All you need is a "+3 baby" layout. The problem is that many double deck games are "No Mid-Deck Entry", or if you *can* jump in, there may be but one or two rounds left before the shuffle.

Getting in Extra Hands: Now, what about when you're already at a crowded table and an impressive flurry of low cards has hit the board? If there's room to play two hands, go ahead and blurt out something like, *"I gotta put in an extra hand to change these cards around -- they're brutal!"* And what if there's no room for an extra hand? Then you might want to trigger the other players' superstitious instincts by making some bizarre play with your hand. Here's what I mean.

Let's say you've got *12* against a dealer's *deuce* with a $40 bet up. Well, you know you're going to take exactly one hit and then stand no matter what you catch. Doing that, you'll lose this hand five times out of eight *(after adjusting for ties)*. There's absolutely nothing you can do about it. But there *is* something else you can do that might improve your odds. What is it?

DOUBLE FOR "LESS" BY SHOVING
AN EXTRA $1 CHIP OUT THERE!

What can a rum-dum move like that possibly do for you?

1) The dealer will announce to the floor, *"Doubling on hard 12."*
2) The players will look at you as if you're an idiot and;
3) If the dealer ends up making a winning hand, one or two

players may very well sit out the rest of the shoe or even leave the table -- *and that will be their own fault!* Now you'll get to take more hands from that favorable shoe with bigger bets before the shuffle comes. And what will it have cost you?

Remember, I said you'll lose the hand five times out of eight? That's like doing it eight times, winning three and losing five for an extra loss of $2 on the eight hands combined. It's a 25 cent per hand additional loss over and above what you must lose just by being stuck with *12* against a *deuce*. So for an averaged cost of 25 cents, you might get in five or six extra hands at $40 or $60 or maybe even $100 apiece with an edge working on every one of them!

IT'S ALL IN HAVING THE RIGHT KIND OF CARD SENSE --

-- the card sense to understand that you want to receive as many hands as you can from shoes or decks that contain a significant surplus of high cards.

Other hands that you might try to "thin out" the table with by doubling for an extra dollar are with *12* against a dealer's *3* or *4* up. They carry just about the same cost penalty. But there are still two *additional* hands you can double for the *full amount* with, and the beauty is -- *they'll both be the correct play for the situation!* Yet, they're apt to agitate players at your table into leaving. What are they?

Remember the *Magnificent 7 Hands?* When the board contains a flock of extra *babies,* it's to your advantage to double down with *Ace/7* against a *2* or with *Ace/8* against a *6!* At a crowded table with a heavy shoe, either of these two doubles might easily serve the dual purpose of earning you extra money while thinning out the table for the upcoming advantageous rounds!

This chapter on grooming your game beyond basic strategy has shown you only those refinements that do not require you to be a card counter *per se.* Even using them all though, you'll have a tough time trying to erase that last $1/2\%$ disadvantage. But if you can reduce a 0.5% disadvantage to a 0.2% disadvantage *(which is entirely feasible using the fine-tuning methods in this chapter),* then a

115

$1000 loss for the year becomes a $400 loss. And your roughly 30% chance to actually have a winning year *(playing 3 or 4 hours a week)* improves to over 40%!

I'm afraid that without keeping track of at least *some* cards right from the first hand dealt, this is just about all you can do to raise the level of your play. ***But wait!*** There is however, one really simple, easy way to keep track of just the *critical* cards and gain a very small overall edge in the game doing it. And the best part is;

YOU ONLY HAVE TO KEEP TRACK FOR THE FIRST HALF DOZEN ROUNDS OR SO IN A SHOE GAME!

Once the shoe gets to that point, you can forget about counting -- *and just play.* Doing this, you can actually erase that last $1/2$% disadvantage and gain $1/4$% percent the best of it -- overall! If you want to cross over from underdog to favorite at blackjack, *that would be the very least you could do.*

Interested? Skeptical? Then, why not turn the page and see just how straightforward and easy casing a shoe can really be.

Chapter 6
KEY POINTS

1) For basic strategy players, blackjack is a game of rote. But just beyond that, it begins to involve personal analysis.

2) In some single and double deck games, an observant player can recognize an advantageous Insurance bet.

3) Just going by a basic strategy chart, you'd think that all hands with the same total are identical. But some hands, particularly 16's, can often be played more effectively by noticing which cards the 16 contains. This goes beyond plain basic strategy.

4) In other cases as well, the mere presence of just a few extra high or low cards on the board can also make it correct to play your hand differently from the basic strategy.

5) You can often gain an edge by partaking in other players' advantageous hands when they elect not to extract the maximum gain.

6) Sometimes it's easy to recognize a shoe that has turned "positive" for the players -- or more negative than usual and to react effectively to both.

7) When you find a positive shoe, you can sometimes "hog" it to yourself by triggering the other players' superstitious instincts to leave the table.

8) Doing all these things can reduce your disadvantage to practically nil. But if you want to gain an overall edge at blackjack, you simply must keep a tally of at least a few key cards. Luckily, there is one really simple way to do this -- and it's presented in the following chapter.

117

SECTION D

Gaining the Edge

WARNING:
BEFORE YOU COMMIT

Playing refined basic strategy with consistent bets brings linear results and reasonable volatility. But with card counting, *that all changes big time!*

Your bet sizes will need to vary dramatically, causing **violent swings!** Sooner or later, you'll run into a prolonged losing streak where all your chips will vanish quickly and repeatedly. No hand will be good enough! Every dealer will have super-human drawing powers -- *and it will seem to never end!*

If you can't outlast such a streak, **then card counting is not for you!** Just play basic strategy. You'll be a contender – *until they grind you down.*

However, if you do have the endurance and the money to absorb card counting's nasty swings, that ugly streak *will* eventually end. And you'll most likely end up beating blackjack. So if you think you're up to that, **read on!**

2017 UPDATE

***SPECIAL NOTE TO READERS:** This chapter was originally written and its strategy was developed with a "*stand on soft 17*" game in mind, which was prevalent back in the early 2000's. Here in 2017, most lower and medium stakes games now *hit soft 17*. That will cut about $^2/_{10}$% off the *Ace/Ten Front Count's* "out-of-the-box" yield and reduce it to a practically break even system. It'll still eliminate the basic strategy house advantage, but be aware that the figures and percentages stated in this chapter apply to a *stand on soft 17* game. To win outright with the *Ace/Ten Front Count* in a *hit soft 17* game, it is strongly recommended that you adopt at least one additional checkpoint deeper in the shoe, as outlined on page 128.

7

the *Ace/10* *Front Count*

This chapter is set apart from the card counting segment of the book because it's not actually card counting in the traditional sense. Conventional card counting requires you to keep track of various high and low cards, beginning with the first hand dealt and running all the way through to the shuffle.

The *Ace/10 Front Count* is a much more basic tool that you simply use to gauge the "high/low" strength of a six deck shoe *at the point where the first two decks have been dealt.* That's its primary purpose. Using it as a barometer, you'll know when to bet more money the rest of the way -- and when to leave the table.

The *Ace/10 Front Count* is nowhere near as difficult to learn, nor as potent as a full-fledged card counting system but;

*FOLLOWING IT RELIGIOUSLY CAN GIVE
YOU THE OVERALL EDGE IN THE GAME

by a very slight margin. This is true even though *you only need to keep track of things for the first part of the shoe!*

The reason this method works is because you and the dealer play according to somewhat different rules and restrictions.

And those differences make *high cards* more valuable to the player than to the dealer *(a thorough and detailed explanation of this axiom is presented in Chapter 8)*. So if you're serious about being a winner at blackjack, you **must** realize that the **key** is having some awareness of the current supply of high vs. low cards.

Here's how the *Ace/10 Front Count* works. You must begin at the top of a fresh six deck shoe. The only cards you pay any attention to are the **10's, Jacks, Queens, Kings** and *Aces* -- that's it. This is not a "plus/minus" count -- but something much simpler! All you do is add together all the *10's* and *Aces* that were dealt out during the first two decks -- *no further!* That's why it's *called a "front count"*.

Do this by starting off at "zero", and counting forward with each *10* or *Ace* that appears. *Once two decks are in the discard tray, you stop counting altogether and just play the rest of the shoe out according to how many Ace/10's there are in the four decks that remain.*

NOW, HOW HARD CAN THAT BE?

To show you how logical and straightforward the *Ace/10 Front Count* is, let's take you through a dry run. Suppose that right off the top of the shoe, the first round of cards consists of:

That's four *Ace/10's* that have been played so far. Now, if the second round is:

called a "front count": With a six deck shoe, things usually don't get very far out of balance before the first two decks are dealt. If you're going to pick just one checkpoint at which to rate the "playability" of the remaining pack, this would be it. Once those front two decks are gone, you'll typically get about 2¼ more decks to play before the shuffle.

your front count will have climbed to "9". Since there are sixteen *10's* and four *Aces* in each full deck of cards, you'll often see about forty *Ace/10's* in the first two dealt decks -- *but not always!*

Although forty *Ace/10's* would be normal, about 20% of the time significantly fewer *Ace/10's* will come out leaving a valuable surplus in the shoe. *That's when you should bet bigger the rest of the way through, while making some advanced plays with a few of your hands.* Other times, there will be an *Ace/10* shortage left, and you should bet very small, or not play at all. It's that darned simple! More specifically;

ANYTIME 36 OR FEWER Ace/10's COME OUT IN THE 1st TWO DECKS, YOU'LL HAVE AN EDGE OVER THE HOUSE

Gauging Two Decks: How will you know when two decks have been dealt? The *discard tray* will be your gauge. Learn to recognize what a two deck stack of cards looks like. Get two decks of "Bee" cards, stack them together and focus on their thickness. You'll find that they stand just about 1.2 inches tall. Next, add some more cards, then try to cut out exactly two decks. Test yourself repeatedly. You must consistently come within three or four cards of 104 -- or you're *not accurate enough*!

121

---

not accurate enough: If you counted 36 *Ace/10s* when you think two decks (104 cards) have been played, but only 96 cards have actually come out, a normal count would be "37" and not "40". That puts only one extra *Ace/10* in the shoe, not four, and you've still got a small disadvantage! So practice until you have it down cold.

Now let's stop and think for a minute about what a front count of "36" after two played decks means. It means there are four extra *Ace/10's* in the remaining four decks. It also means four extra smaller cards were removed to make room for the surplus *10's* and *Aces (providing you've eyeballed the discard tray accurately enough).* Instead of having a $1/2\%$ *disadvantage*, you now have a $1/3\%$ *advantage!* You can simply stop counting and bet higher the rest of the way through the shoe!

Is this a legitimate strategy to follow? *Yes it is!* If you think about it, it's exactly the same as the dealer putting in a fresh four deck pack and informing you that it has "so many" *Aces* and *10's* in it rather than the normal total of 80. What you're doing is appropriately tailoring your wagers to just how many *Ace/10's* that particular four deck shoe contains. It's true that as the rest of the shoe plays out, it may grow proportionally richer in *Ace/10's* or leaner, but on average;

YOU'LL BE DEALT ENOUGH EXTRA Ace/10's
FROM THAT REMAINING SHOE TO TURN A PROFIT

Don't forget that when you play strict basic strategy the shoe is continuously growing richer and leaner too -- but you still keep playing your hands as though the shoe is the same as it was at the start. The thing to understand about this concept is; *whatever the shoe is **right now** has become the new norm, and things will tend to centralize themselves around that the rest of the way.*

HOW TO BEGIN

Okay, let's say you want to put the *Ace/10 Front Count* into action. Simply walk out onto the blackjack floor and look for a table where the dealer is shuffling so that you can start at the top of a fresh shoe. *But wait!* Don't step up to the table yet. Instead....

REMAIN IN THE BACKGROUND AND WATCH
THE FIRST TWO DECKS OF THE SHOE COME
OUT WHILE TALLYING UP THE Ace/10's

You're going to take one shot at finding a "36" or under front count before you sit down. *This is important!* If you get what you're looking for, you'll buy in and start betting multiple units right off the bat. However, four times out of five, your front count will be "37" or higher and you'll pass on this table altogether. Now walk over to the next table that's starting a new shoe and just plop right down and play -- *right off the top*. You took your shot at finding an edge going in and it didn't happen. You'll repeat this same effort again when the shoe you're playing tells you that it's time. Meanwhile, you'll be playing and counting the *Ace/10's* from the get-go at this new table. When the discard tray gets two decks thick, here's what you can expect to find:

A) Roughly 55% of the time, you'll get a front count between '37' and '42'. Here, your disadvantage will average only about $1/3$%.

B) About 25% of the time, your front count will be "43" or higher. At these times, your disadvantage will range from 1% to about 3% -- and you'll be aware of it.

C) The remaining 20% of the time or so, your front count will be "36" or under and you'll have an *outright advantage*, ranging from $1/3$% up to over 2%. *This is the shoe you came to find!* Even though you'll get beat on plenty of these, in the big picture it's where you'll make your money. Now here's a specific game plan:

1) If you're playing from the beginning of the shoe, bet one unit through the first two decks and count up all all the *Ace/10's* that come out up to that point.

2) If that front count is '**37**' to '**42**', stick to a one unit bet and finish the shoe.

3) If your front count is "**43**" or higher, **leave the table!** Get up and go find another new shoe -- **but don't play it -- yet!** Front count it first. If it's '36' or under -- **then** you can sit down. If it's not, go to yet another

123

new shoe, sit right down and play. You **must** always give yourself one opportunity to convert a "43 or higher" front count directly into a "36 or lower" count before settling for a full six deck shoe.

4) If your front count is **"36"**, bet **four** units the rest of the way through the shoe and make the following advanced plays with your hands:

DEALER'S UP-CARD

	2	5	6	10	A
9	Double				
11					Double
16				Stand	
A/7	Double				
A/8		Double	Double		

(Play your hands and bet your money in this exact same way whenever you've front counted a shoe from the aisle and gotten a '36' count. Just come right in betting four units until the shuffle).

5) If your front count is **35** or less, bet **six** units the rest of the way and make the following two *additional* plays:

DEALER'S UP-CARD

	3	6
8		Double
12	Stand	

(Also come in betting six units and making all eight special plays anytime you've gotten a '35' or under front count from the aisle).

6) Whenever your front count is **"32"** or less, *take Insurance* every time the dealer's got an Ace up – *regardless* of what hand you have.

Following the prescribed game plan, for every dozen shoes that will cross your path:

> *You'll play 5 of them all the way from start to finish*
> *You'll walk away from 2 after playing the first two decks*
> *You'll jump into 1 after front counting it from the aisle*
> *You'll pass altogether on 4 after scouting the first 2 decks*

That may seem like a lot of bobbing and weaving, but;

THIS SELF-DISCIPLINE IS MANDATORY IF YOU WANT TO GAIN THAT PRECIOUS, MINISCULE EDGE OVER THE HOUSE

using such a simple system. And another thing; when you increase your bets from one to four units, do it in two steps. Go to two units on the next hand and then to four on the following one. When increasing it to six units, first jump to a three unit bet and finally to six. This is to not appear to the pit people as though you might have some idea what you're doing. And remember, keep your bets at the prescribed level -- *win, lose or draw!* This is not a betting progression. You're betting according to your chances of winning the *next* hand. Whether you happened to win or lose the *last* one is irrelevant.

Customized Basic Strategy: Now let me put your mind at ease about straying from your normal basic strategy. Remember what basic strategy is. It gives you your best play assuming that 30% of the cards are *10's*. But what's proper basic strategy for a game like *Spanish 21?* There, you should actually hit *14* against a *deuce!* Why? Because in *Spanish 21*, only 25% of the cards are *10's!* It has it's *own* basic strategy. Well, a four deck pack of cards with 84 or 85 *Ace/10's* left in it *(rather than 80)* has its own proper basic strategy too, and it includes all the plays outlined in this chapter. Let's use the following hand as an example.

Normally when you have *12* against a *3*, there are five cards *(any 5, 6, 7, 8 or 9)* that will make you *17* thru *21* for every four cards that will bust you if you hit. That fact combined with the dealer having only four chances out of thirteen to be holding a *13* make hitting this hand a modestly better play than standing. But when your *front count* is "35", there is a higher proportion of *10's* available to bust you and fewer *5's* thru *9's* to make you a hand. At the same time, the dealer is more likely to be stiff with *13*. With this shoe composition, *you're better off standing!*

What's it all Worth?:
The *Ace/10 Front Count* is the flat out simplest way I know of to get a high/low "read" on a six deck shoe. But what can it do for you in dollars and cents? Well, suppose you were say, a $17 average bettor. By that I mean you vary your bets from $10 up to maybe $25 or $30 such that they average out to $17 each. If you play perfect basic strategy at those stakes, your *long range* expectation is to *lose* about $8 for every hour you've spent at the blackjack tables *(not including tips)*.

Now, playing the *Ace/10 Front Count* to the letter and betting $10-$40-$60, your average bet will also work out to be about $17. But your $1/4\%$ overall *edge* puts your *long range* expectation at a *profit* of around $4 per hour.

Now for the Luck Factor:
Yeah, I know all these figures sound trivial and you've experienced swings much larger than a few dollars per hour betting $15 or $20 per hand. The truth about gambling is, *luck will play a big part in how you'll do on any given day.*

If you play a five hour basic strategy session at $17 per hand, mathematically you're *supposed* to lose $40. But due to the "luck factor" *(statisticians refer to it as "standard deviation")*, you're not that unlikely to actually *win* say, $200. However, you're just as likely to *lose* $280! Both outcomes are the same distance from your expected result, and each will end up occurring about as often as the other.

Playing the *Ace/10 Front Count* for the same five hours on a $10-$40-$60 scale, the math says you're *supposed* to win $20. In reality, *anything* could happen. But this time, you're just as likely to win $320 as lose the $280 -- and over time, that's what tends to put you on the plus side of the game!

That comparison colors the landscape of gambling about as vividly as I know how to paint it. In fact, I'd be remiss if I didn't keep reminding you that even though you'll have a tiny edge;

YOU CAN ALWAYS LOSE!

You might play the *Ace/10 Front Count* along side your brother-in-law who just plays basic strategy, and maybe he'll *win* $500 while you *lose* the "nickel". That's just the nature of the beast. But if the two of you play side by side time after time, you're a big favorite to come out better than your brother-in-law.

Harsh Reality: Now you can see that you'll probably make more money stocking shelves at your local supermarket than playing the *Ace/10 Front Count* for $17 per hand, average. The real point however is that;

IT STILL BEATS THE SNOT OUT OF LOSING JUST LIKE EVERYBODY ELSE!

Sound like a waste of effort? Remember the alternative. Playing basic strategy at $17 per hand, you should be $800 *down* after 100 hours at the tables. Playing the *Ace/10 Front Count*, you should be $400 *up*. With basic strategy your chance of being ahead of the game at this point due to above average cards is about 33%. With the *Front Count* it's 55%. Either way it's still a gamble. But if you figure to continue playing blackjack in the coming years anyway, it ought to be worth taking your game to this next level. *It's your call.*

It really doesn't take much to pick up that extra percentage. All you need to do is know how to count up to 43, recognize a two deck stack of cards when you see one, change your bet size and memorize a few special plays for your hands. If you're an accomplished basic strategy player and are looking for a simple step over the threshold from underdog to favorite, *it just doesn't get any simpler than this!*

How Many Bullets do you Need?: When you were just a recreational blackjack player and never kept track of any cards whatsoever, whether you thought so or not, *you were just trying to get lucky.* If you busted out -- you busted out. But beginning

127

with the *Ace/10 Front Count,* you actually have a super-tiny edge. If you bust out now – no more edge! Now it's time to legitimately finance your play. Gambling is volatile. If you play short-stacked, the swings will bust you – edge or no edge. *To play a three or four hour session you need to walk into the casino with a dozen top bets in your pocket.* At $10-$40-$60 stakes, that's $700! To bet $100-$400-$600 takes $7000. And about one day out of ten, *you'll lose it all!* Fifteen top bets will last you about 95% of the time.

2017 UPDATE

Upgrading the A/10 Count: By initial design, the *Ace/10 Front Count* was merely a single checkpoint shoe casing device for a *stand on soft 17* game. But as years go by, more and more tables are *hitting on soft 17*. **This will reduce the Front Count's net yield to nearly a break even game.** To regain the outright advantage in a *hit soft 17* game using the *Ace/10 Count,* you'll need to track the *Ace/10s* deeper into the shoe – *at least to the three dealt deck mark.*

Just as before, you'll take inventory after the first two decks and make any adjustments. But then, *keep your running total going as the shoe progresses.* When *three* decks have hit the discard tray:

IF YOUR *A/10* COUNT IS '57', BET FOUR UNITS NO MATTER WHAT YOU'VE BEEN BETTING THUS FAR

Also, bet *six* units at '56' or less -- but if it's '58' or more, regress to one unit. Doing this, you won't get trapped into making big bets if a "heavy" shoe turns "lean" further on in. You'll also be able to seize other occasions when a neutral situation turns heavy. This increased betting efficiency will make up for their hitting *soft 17.*

To go 'full bore' with *Ace/10 Count,* you could adopt a third checkpoint at the four deck mark. But beware; eyeballing four decks in the discard tray is tough. If your guess is more than four cards off, your betting will be off too! To go this far, you may just want a signaling partner to count down 104, 156 and 208 cards for you. At the four deck mark, *bet four units at a count of '77'.* Bet *six* units at '76' or less – but if it's '78' or more, just bet one unit.

Updating your count at the three deck mark *(while maintaining those critical entering/exiting rules)* will yield about a $^2/_{10}$% net edge in a *hit soft 17* game, and $^1/_3$% with *stand soft 17.* Adding a four deck checkpoint will yield about $^1/_3$% with *H17* and $^1/_2$% with *S17.*

128

Optimizing Your Play: Front counts of '37' or '38' leave you about a break even shoe to play going forward. So the right time to hit the john, break to eat or quit for the day is at a front count of '39' or higher. That'll eliminate some action you were about to put in as an underdog. It makes more sense than playing out that shoe.

Playing '36-or-under' front counts is *key*. The more trouble you take to count down new shoes from the aisle, the better you'll do. Sure, you came to play – not walk around. But you came to *win*, first and foremost. The "heavy" shoes are *where the money is!*

Chapter 7
KEY POINTS

1) With a six deck shoe, you usually need to deal out the first couple of decks before the remaining pack turns notably advantageous or more disadvantageous to the player.

2) By tallying up all the Ace/10s that appear in those first two decks, a player can assess his winning chances for that shoe.

3) To obtain a slight winning edge, it's not necessary to track the cards beyond the first two or three decks.

4) Just by using his "front two deck tally", the player will know whether to increase his wagers for the rest of the shoe, keep them the same -- or even leave the table.

5) That same information will tell the player when it's proper to make some unusual, advanced plays with his hands.

6) By standing back and watching the distribution of the first two decks from the aisle, a player can also determine whether to come in and play, or to just "pass" on that table.

7) About 20% of the six deck shoes turn "positive" for the player by the time two decks are dealt.

8) About one-fourth of the six deck shoes turn prohibitively "negative" for the player by the time two decks are dealt.

9) By betting four to six times as much money on the positive shoes and by walking away from the negative ones, the player can gain about a $1/4$% net edge in the game.

129

8

the *"High Card /*
Low Card" Axiom

A key ingredient that sets blackjack apart from other casino-banked table games is the fact that the controls are not set back to square one after each bet is settled. If somebody was just dealt two pair in Caribbean stud, it really doesn't make a bit of difference after the deck is shuffled and they start to deal the next hand. The odds against receiving another two pair hand are still, and always will be 20-to-1.

But in blackjack, several hands are dealt between shuffles. This is a major factor to the truly diligent *"21"* player. That's because the odds of being dealt good hands or bad hands vary as the cards are played out.

If you've been around the game of blackjack any length of time at all, I'm sure you've heard it said somewhere that high cards, like *10's* and *Aces* favor the player. Is this just an old piece of gambling folklore, or is there something to it?

Well, there's a *lot* to it! *Not only do high cards favor the player, but low cards help the dealer big time!* Now, some people's response to this statement might be, *"Yeah, but when a lot of high cards are left, doesn't the dealer have the same chance of getting a 10 or an Ace as the player?"* Yes he does; exactly the same chance. But the player can do a lot more with high cards than the dealer can. That's because as pointed out in Chapter 2 *(the House Edge),* the player and dealer don't really play by quite the same rules. Sure, they're both trying to make *"21",* but that's where the similarity ends.

As you know, the player may hit or stand at will, while the dealer *must* hit *16* or less. But are you aware that the basic strategy player *voluntarily* elects to *stand* on 35% of his stiffs *(12 through 16)?* The dealer however, must hit them *all,* even if he already has your *13* beaten with *16!* This makes small cards very useful to the dealer.

Here's a question for you. What's the most valuable card in the deck for the dealer? Many people will say it's the *deuce,* because they seem to lose so many heartbreaking hands to a dealer's *deuce* up. But actually, the most precious card for the dealer is the;

It's true, when the dealer has a *5* up she's at her weakest, but if she turns up 12 through 16;

CATCHING A 5 WILL TURN EVERY
DEALER'S STIFF INTO A MADE HAND

Notice that by drawing a *5,* any *12* becomes *17* and a *16* becomes *21.* That's a pretty sweet ending for someone who's *forced* to play Russian Roulette! In fact, computer analysis studies have shown that the *5* is the most important card in the entire game, mostly because it bails the dealer out of so many tight spots. The next most useful cards to the dealer are the *4* and then the *6.*

Conversely, only the player receives a 1 1/2 to 1 payoff for his blackjacks which makes those *10's* and *Aces* more valuable to him. Also, the player can split up lousy pairs like *Aces* or *8's.*

131

Here again, a high card would come in handy. And finally, the player is usually rooting for a big card when doubling down. In fact, when there are lot of *10's* in the deck, even the Insurance bet becomes an advantage to the player. Indeed, most of the options that are exclusively available to the player are enhanced by the presence of high cards.

So what's the most valuable card in the deck for the player? The *9* is a *little* bit of help, but for top honors it's a real close call between the *10* and the *Ace*. The more of these there are, the more times the player will be able to take advantage of his right to double down, split and of course, get paid a bonus on his blackjacks.

FANTASTIC RULES IN SPANISH "21"

To give you an idea how important high cards are to the player, let's look at the relatively new game of *"Spanish 21"*. It has terrific rules. The player's blackjack beats a dealer's blackjack. A player's *21* beats the dealer's *21*. You can double down on any two, three or four cards. You can surrender half your double bet after you double down if you don't like the card you caught. You can take extra hits to your split *Aces*. And there are some bonuses for special hands like *7-7-7* or a five card *21* among other perks. How can they do this? They take all the;

out of the deck! The *Jacks, Queens* and *Kings* remain, thus *the shoe has been depleted of 25% of its 10-counters*. You could *never* offer those rules with a fully stocked pack of cards.

TRY PINOCHLE BLACKJACK

Still need more convincing? Then you owe it to yourself to walk over to the kitchen table and deal yourself some blackjack with a pinochle deck, where the smallest card is a *9*. Take full advantage of all those high cards by splitting *10's* every time the dealer has a *9* showing. Double down with *Ace/9* against a *9* up and always take Insurance. Keep score for 40 or 50 hands. It it'll become obvious what's happening.

You see, with no cards smaller than a *9*, everybody is always dealt a pat hand, except for a pair of Aces. You can never bust *(except by suicide)!* That *was* the dealer's sole advantage -- that he always takes your money immediately when you bust, even if he breaks later in the hand himself. With all else being equal, it would now be an even game. Aah, ***but all else is not equal!***

Why not? For one thing, the dealer can still bust. How? What about when he turns over this hand?

If *you* have a pair of *Aces*, you get to hit *11* twice by splitting, and the deck is loaded with *10's!* You'll *never* bust and your average finishing hand will be 19^2/3 *(with a pinochle deck)*. But the *dealer* has to hit a soft *12!* Virtually the only way he can *avoid* busting is to catch a *9* in there somewhere.

Besides that, you still get paid 1^1/2 to 1 on your blackjacks. And now, your blackjacks will come once every 4^1/2 hands instead of the normal once in 21 hands. And you still can split pairs and double down in those spots where it is to your advantage to do so.

Plus, now the Insurance wager favors the player instead of the house! Why? Because you'll win two out of every three Insurance bets collecting 2 units for each win, and losing 1 unit for your loss. And the dealer will have an *Ace* up once every 6 hands instead of one time in 13.

WITH A PINOCHLE DECK, BLACKJACK ISN'T EVEN CLOSE!

And the closer a blackjack deck gets to being a pinochle deck, the more it favors the player. *Is this making sense?*

Still have your doubts about high cards in blackjack? Okay, then you're a prime candidate for the ultimate acid test. How about a nice private game of "Strip-Blackjack" with your significant other using a pinochle deck? You be the big, bad "invincible" dealer; let your mate be the poor "defenseless" player. But don't get your hopes up too high 'cause -- you're the one who'll be stark naked in no time!

Okay, so maybe high cards *do* help the player. So what? Well, the obvious thing would be to bet more when a lot of high cards are left in the deck, or shoe. In a 6 deck game the distribution of high and low cards remains pretty even about 60% of the time. During these stretches, the house enjoys an edge of about 1/2%. Another 20% of the time, there are a lot of little cards left and the house advantage swells to an average of about 2%. During the remaining 20% of the time, there's a surplus of high cards and the *player* actually has an advantage averaging about 1%.

With a single deck, the shifting percentages are more dramatic. The player will have the advantage on the next hand about one-third of the time, and by a larger margin. Why is this? Since the player only has an edge when the composition of remaining cards gets out of kilter, the fewer cards that are involved, the more easily it can happen.

Picture that this way. Let's say you were going to flip three coins in the air, and in order to win they had to come down at least two-thirds heads. This would happen successfully 50% of the time. But if you threw 30 coins into the air and still needed two-thirds heads, you'd only get the 20 needed heads 5% of the time. You see, with so many more coins falling, the distribution of heads and tails would hang closer to 50-50. *This is how the house begins to insulate itself from card counters when they use multi-deck shoes.*

Anyway, be it one deck or eight, by staying aware of the condition of the remaining pack, card counters can bet more when they have the advantage, and less the rest of the time. If you can

134

bet more money when you have the advantage than you did all the rest of the times that you were at a disadvantage, then you become the overall favorite in the game!

Being the favorite however, is not the same thing as winning. Pay close attention to the small edges we're working with here. Lot's of rookie card counters think when a strong count has them betting it up, winning is a "done deal". This is far from true. You'll never get to play with cards nearly as "rich" as a pinochle deck.

In multi-deck shoe games, you'll seldom have more than a couple percent edge on that big bet you've just made. Sometimes you'll count through a half dozen shoes waiting to find an opportunity to put some real money out there, and when it finally comes you'll lose five or six big bets in a row. Add in a couple of tips for the dealer, then lose your concentration a few times and;

IT CAN BE A PRETTY "IFFY" WAY
TO MAKE SOME EASY MONEY

This is the nature of gambling. You'll have the edge for sure -- but winning is merely *probable*. The longer you play with that edge though, the more probable winning becomes.

The *Ace/10 Front Count* from the previous chapter showed you an entirely *recreational* method of tracking high cards to give you a tiny edge at blackjack. Starting with the next chapter, you'll be shown how to increase your edge beyond that point -- *one step at a time*. Your next rung on the ladder is to learn a simple way to keep your high card/low card information up-to-date all the way through the shoe. For that purpose, an *entry level* plus/minus system which tracks only half of all the dealt cards is next up. It's called the *KISS Count*.

Chapter 8
KEY POINTS

1) The key ingredient which makes blackjack mathematically beatable is that the controls are not set back to square one by shuffling after each hand is played.

2) Since the rules are somewhat different for the player than for the dealer, high cards help the player win money while low cards help the house.

3) By being aware of when the remaining cards are predominantly high, the player can gain an edge if he bets more money at those times.

4) The fact that high cards do indeed help the player is evidenced by the development of new blackjack games with super-loose rules and some 10's removed from the pack.

5) The advantage that high cards afford the player can be easily demonstrated, simply by playing blackjack for a short while with a Pinochle deck -- where the smallest card is a 9.

9

the "KISS" *Card Count*

What percentage of all the blackjack players would you say play reasonably sound basic strategy? Maybe 25%? And what percentage are card counters? I'm sure it's well under 1%. Why such a difference? I don't have to tell you it's because counting cards is much more demanding than just playing basic strategy. Yet, memorizing your basic strategy chart to a tee still can't give you the advantage in the game -- but counting just *some* of the cards *can* if you do things right.

The *Ace/10 Front Count (from Chapter 7)* was an extremely *basic* and *borderline* approach to winning play. If it had been placed here in the thick of the card counting section, players who don't wish to become card counters would probably never see it. But I wanted serious basic strategy players to at least have an introductory glimpse at what advantage play is about. As you know, the name of the game is to:

GET THE SERIOUS MONEY OUT THERE WHEN THERE ARE MORE HIGH CARDS LEFT THAN LOW CARDS

On that point, the *Ace/10 Front Count* is a legitimate advantage strategy. But its major shortcoming is that it has no idea when a "rich" shoe *(lots of high cards)* may turn "lean" and you should therefore be cutting back your bets. To be "up to snuff" on that, you simply have to keep on tracking the cards as the pack plays out! That's the part that separates real card counting from a "single checkpoint" strategy like the *Ace/10 Front Count.*

Now, "real" card counting systems have been around for a long time. In general, they are not a recreational tool. These count systems keep methodical track of most of the cards that have been played -- all the way through to the shuffle. In doing so, they can convert a $1/2\%$ basic strategy disadvantage into about a $3/4\%$ net edge in a typical shoe game. That would be a $11/4\%$ overall shift in the percentages. To master one of these systems requires at least scores, if not hundreds of hours of practice. Very few blackjack players are both willing and able to persevere to that level of expertise with a full scale card count -- which is why there are so few card counters out there.

KEEPING IT SIMPLE

The funny thing about card counting systems though, is that they produce this oddity called, *"rapidly diminishing returns".* What it means is;

TRACKING JUST A FEW KEY CARDS HELPS THE MOST

Adding a few more cards to the list improves the results less than the first few -- and adding even more cards improves things still less. The thing of it is, ***you really don't need to track that many cards to gain a valuable advantage in the game!***

That's where the *KISS Count* comes in. It stands for; *"Keep It Simple, Stupid".* You see, you can actually gain most of that $11/4\%$ shift by tracking only *half* the cards in the deck or shoe -- *if you follow the right cards.* According to my computer simulation runs involving roughly two billion hands, the *KISS Count* can convert a $1/2\%$ six deck basic strategy disadvantage into a $1/2\%$ net edge! And it does so by counting exactly half the cards that get dealt out.

Here's how the *KISS Count* works. We already know that in blackjack, some cards affect the odds of the game more than others. Now, the three most significant *low* cards in blackjack are the *4*, the *5* and the *6*   Among *high* cards, the *10's* and *Aces* are all vital -- but you can get a fairly good read on what's happening just by following the most obvious high ones, like the *picture cards* for example. If you're not going all out for maximum gain, you can afford to ignore the *10-spots* and the *Aces* along with several other less important cards.   In addition, the *KISS Count* employs one other "automating" feature *(explained later)* which makes it more user friendly at the expense of minimal accuracy. The following graphic lays out the *KISS Count* in visual form:

The KISS Card Count

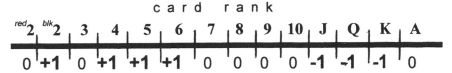

So that's 3^1/$_2$ ranks of low cards you'll need to follow along with 3 ranks of high cards. *The rest, you can forget.* The most popular counting systems out there today keep track of 10 or 11 ranks. In doing so, they are about **97%** efficient at recognizing advantageous deck compositions *(this is called a system's "betting correlation")*. The *KISS Count* has a **79%** betting correlation. So by monitoring the distribution of about 60% as many cards as a full scale count system, the *KISS Count* is about 80% as efficient. That's what is meant by "rapidly diminishing returns".

THE COUNTING PROCESS

When counting cards, you must always begin off the top of a *fresh* deck, or shoe. If you're playing against a **single** deck, begin your count before you see the first card with the number "18" in your mind. That'll be your starting point. For other decks.............

:In **double** deck play;	begin at "17"
:With **four** decks;	begin at "14"
:With a **six** deck shoe;	begin at "10"
:With **eight** decks;	begin at "6"

This will be called your *Initial Running Count.*

139

Now - every time a **4**, **5**, **6** or ***black deuce*** comes out, add one point to your total. And with each ***face-card*** that is dealt, subtract one point from your total. Just ignore any *3's, 7's, 8's, 9's, 10-spots, Aces or red deuces! Got that?*

Okay, let's practice counting a few cards. You've just taken a seat at a table where they're dealing from a six deck shoe. The dealer is shuffling, so clear your mind and pre-load your count by putting the number **"10"** in your head. Place your minimum bet *(because the house always has the advantage on the first hand off the top of a fresh shoe).* There are two other players at the table with you. Here comes the first hand:

The cards you count here are the *Jack,* the *6,* the *4* and the dealer's *5. **Ignore all the other ones even though they may matter.*** They are not within the scope of this "entry-level" count system. Your running count would now be **"12"**. Let's say that the next three cards to get turned up were all *8's* to finish the hand -- leaving your running count still at **"12"**. Now, if the next round of cards was;

140

you would count the *King,* the *Queen* and the *deuce of spades* to put your running count at **"11"**. Do *not* count the *deuce of hearts* or the *10!* Three consecutive *8's* again were then exposed as the hands played out to finish up this round. Okay now, *you* tell *me;* after all the cards below came out on the next couple of rounds, what would your running count be?

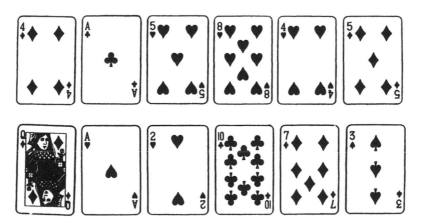

Look carefully. If you didn't get a count of **"14"**, go back and check again. When you're playing, be sure to notice every card

141

that gets turned up. Don't worry about missing the burn card at the beginning of the deal, or one that may get burned while the dealers are switched at your table. It's not enough to make a significant difference. Any burned card is in the same category as all those behind the plastic cut-off card; *unknown* and theoretically available.

PRACTICE, PRACTICE, PRACTICE

Don't be silly enough to think you can learn this in the casino. You have to drill yourself at home. Practice counting with a single deck by turning the cards over one at a time, in as rapid succession as you can without making a mistake. For practicing, start off your count at **"18"**. When you have one card left, *stop! Can you name the category of the last card?* There are 3 choices;

A) *a **4, 5, 6** or **black deuce***
B) *a **picture card***
C) *a **"no-counter"***

Since you've been counting those two *black deuces* with no high cards to cancel them out on the other side, your running count should rise by two points to **"20"** after you get through a complete deck. So, if your count with one card left is **"19"**, then the last card should be a *4, 5, 6* or *black deuce.* If your count is **"21"**, the last card is a *picture.* And if your count is already **"20"**, then the final card is a *"no-counter".* When you can count down a 52 card deck comfortably and accurately *within 30 seconds,* you're ready for casino action.

Why the black deuces?: Wondering why you're counting the *black deuces* but not the red ones? Good question! Traditionally, full blown counting systems have *balanced* card counts. That is, you count the same number of high cards as low cards and begin your count at "0". At any point during the deal then, a "+10" count would mean that ten more low cards have come out than high cards; and a "-10" count would mean just the

opposite. As neat and tidy as that may sound, it's not very "user friendly" in actual play.

The problem is when there are five decks left in the shoe, a "+10" count means there are *two extra high cards* for each deck that remains. But if there are only two decks left, then there are *five extra high cards* per deck. ***These two conditions are not the same thing!*** The second condition is much stronger than the first. So with balanced card counts, you need to divide your running count by the number of decks that remain to find out how strong or weak the high/low ***ratio*** of unplayed cards has become.

The *KISS* system gets around all that by unbalancing its count with the *black deuce*. This is the ***automating feature** mentioned a few pages back. Now you can just keep counting, and if your running count ever reaches **"20"**, you know it's time to raise your bet -- with any number of cards remaining! *The approximate high/low ratio of the remaining cards has been automatically tied to the running count!* Therefore;

YOU NEVER HAVE TO WORRY ABOUT HOW DEEP INTO THE DECK OR SHOE YOU ARE

With a running count of **"20"**, you'll usually have about a $4/10\%$ advantage whether there are five decks left or just two decks. The further above **"20"** the running count climbs, the bigger favorite you are and the more you should bet. Thus, ***recognizing when you have the edge* is a snap with unbalanced card counting *since you do everything strictly by the running count.* The fine print section on the next page explains the mechanics of unbalanced edge-tracking and is optional reading for the inquisitive.

****automating feature**: We have to credit *Arnold Snyder* of *Blackbelt in Blackjack* fame for initiating the idea of splitting up a card rank to obtain the ideal imbalance between high and low cards. His *Red 7 Count*, introduced in the early '80's went unrecognized as the solid performer that it is, until the proliferation of blackjack simulation software several years later. Snyder's count, as the name implies tracks the red 7's, (but not the black ones) along with all the 2's thru 6's as low cards. Pitting those against all the 10's and Aces creates an "auto-calibrating" imbalance that causes the raw running count to be a reasonably accurate indicator of the current high/low strength of unplayed cards at all deck penetration levels. Hence, the need for dividing by the number of remaining decks is eliminated.

**Recognizing the edge: How does unbalanced counting automatically calculate your edge? Let's look at a six deck shoe, where you begin your running count at "10". Suppose that after one deck has been played out, your running count rises to "22". Just how strong would that be? Well, had one intact deck come out, its two black deuces would cause your count to rise to "12". Then everything would still be "even" and you'd again have the standard house disadvantage. But at "22", ten extra little cards have been eliminated -- leaving ten extra picture cards in the shoe. And with five decks remaining, that's *two extra pictures per deck.* Hold onto that thought.

Now let's fast forward to where four decks have gone by, and you again have a running count of "22". How strong is a "22" count now? With two black deuces in each normal deck, everything would be back to even if your count was "18" at this point. But at "22", the remaining shoe is four picture cards heavy. And with just two decks left, that's also *two extra pictures per deck* (a +2 "true count" in card counting lingo). In fact, *any time you have a "22" running count, the remaining cards will be a +2 true count!* I'll leave any additional checkpoints up to you.

No matter whether it's 1, 2, 4, 6 or 8 deck blackjack, you'll always have *exactly* a +2 true count whenever your running count has risen *by "two x the number of starting decks".* As the running count strays away from that point, your count begins to lose accuracy. But +2 true, and all counts near it constitute a critical strategic range that winning play is built upon. Computer simulation runs have shown that unbalanced counts yield about 95% as much net edge as a balanced count of equal structural complexity.

Now, if you never had to worry about the floorman getting his nose out of joint over your wide betting spreads, your *KISS Count* wagering would go something like this:

IDEAL BETTING

RUNNING COUNT	BET SIZE
19 or less	1 unit
20	3 units
21	6 units
22	8 units
23 or more	12 units

Okay, *so much for ideals!* The reality is, with 1 or 2 decks, your running count will bounce back and forth, above and below **"20"** so quickly that you will probably not be able to bet in direct accordance with the chart. If you did, you're "wild" betting would attract undesirable attention from the pit. In "hand held" games, it would be good policy to never more than double your last bet, no matter how sharply the count may rise. It's easiest to do this when you've won the last hand, by letting your winnings ride.

Practical Single Deck Betting: It's probably best to begin off the top of each deck with a *2 unit* wager, then drop to 1 unit if the count is still below **"20"** at the start of the second hand. In that way, it'll be easier to get to the larger bets without such a glaring change in wager size. Even at that, you should almost never bet more than *4 units* -- or the dealer may shuffle abruptly. *This is something you must avoid!* It would be much better to have only 4 units riding on a **"24"** count hand, than to get it shuffled away. In fact, at the higher stakes, any spread wider than *1-to-3* probably won't fly! *You* will have to be the judge of how much betting latitude you can get away with in these games. That's where the *art* of the game comes into play.

Double Deck Betting: In two deck games you should be able to get down your *6 unit* bets okay -- as long as you're not more than doubling your last wager. Here too, it's usually best to start off the top with *2 units*. Then a 6 unit wager later in the deck won't look so huge. And if you finish up a deck with a top sized wager, you'd better yield a little on your edge and start off the next deck with a *3 unit* bet for visibility purposes.

Betting the Shoe Games: In 4 to 8 deck play, everything will oscillate much more gradually. Besides that, pit crews are less paranoid about card counters when multiple decks are used. Consequently, you should have little trouble betting in accordance with the count. In four deck play however, any spread wider than *1-to-9* is probably a bad move. With six decks, *1-to-10* should usually not be exceeded. The eight deckers just plain need *1-to-12,* so you've got to go for it there. Your **"20+"** counts may only occur once every 3 or 4 shoes and will tend to come nearer the shuffle. You need such a wider spread in your betting units when

145

playing the shoe games because you won't have the advantage very often. When you do, you need to get more money on the table than you risked through all those waiting bets. This of course will lead to greater volatility in your results. In a three or four hour playing session, you'll generally find that the outcome of a few hundred hands of blackjack depended upon how you did with maybe a dozen assorted large bets.

Playing the
"ADVANTAGE STRATEGY"

When the running count reaches **"20"**, there is a large enough surplus of face-cards, and a shortage of small ones in the unplayed pack to make the player a money favorite on the next hand. That's why you should raise your bet. Also at these times, *some hands could be played more productively than by simply following the basic strategy.*

The basic strategy is the player's blackjack bible. About 95% of the time it's the right way to go. But the basic strategy has determined the right play based on the assumption that all cards are equally available. However, when your *KISS Count* is **"20"** or higher, all cards are *not* equally available! At these times, the following *six* hands should all be played according to the *"Advantage Strategy"* rather than basic strategy, hand composition or the *10's* vs. *babies* on board! It's called the Advantage Strategy because this will be your playing mode when you have the advantage in the game.

ADVANTAGE STRATEGY HANDS

HAND	Basic Strategy	ADVANTAGE STRATEGY
9 vs. 2 up	hit	DOUBLE
11 vs. Ace	hit	DOUBLE
16 vs. 10 up	hit	STAND
A7 vs. 2 up	stand	DOUBLE
A8 vs. 5 up	stand	DOUBLE
A8 vs. 6 up	stand	DOUBLE

146

Also, be sure to stand with *12* against a *4* and with *13* against a *deuce* even if a flock of *10's* may be on board at the time. A "**20+**" *KISS Count* overrides all previous, more superficial hand playing strategies *because it knows more about the remaining cards than all of them.*

TAKING INSURANCE

By now you know that Insurance is nothing more than a catchy side bet invented by the casino to make more money for the house. How does the house do this? They do it the same way they make money at the craps table by paying 9-to-5 odds for a place bet on the 10 -- when the true odds are 2-to-1 against making that 10. They simply pay you shorter odds than the true odds against winning your bet.

Whenever you take Insurance at the blackjack table, you're simply betting that the dealer has a *10* in the hole, and the house will pay you 2-to-1 odds on your Insurance bet if she has it. But the true odds against the dealer having that *10* in the hole are *usually* 2¹/4-to-1.

USUALLY is the key word here! You see, making a 10 in craps is *always* 2-to-1 against. But the dealer having a *10* underneath her *Ace* is *usually* 2¹/4-to-1! It all depends upon how many *10's* are left in the unplayed cards! Fact is;

**SOMETIMES THE ODDS ARE 2³/4-to-1
AND SOMETIMES THEY'RE 1³/4-to-1**

Whenever the odds are below 2-to-1, the *player* has the edge on the Insurance bet instead of the *house* -- because then he'll be getting *greater* than the true odds!

In a multi-deck shoe game on average, when your *KISS Count* is "**25**", the odds against the dealer having a *10* in the hole will be under 2-to-1. In hand held games, this occurs at a lower number. The following chart tells you at what count you should take Insurance with the *KISS Count*.

INSURANCE REQUIREMENT FOR THE KISS COUNT

DECKS IN USE	MIN. RUNNING COUNT
Single Deck play	"21"
Double Deck games	"22"
4 to 8 Deck shoes	"25"

Whenever you reach any of the above running counts in that particular game, **Take Insurance!** And remember, it doesn't matter what your hand is. You're betting on something else. You'll win or lose your hand just the same. The two bets are not the slightest bit related. You take Insurance at a specified count because you have uncovered an advantageous bet. You are not trying to hedge the bet on your hand.

Okay, now you have three things to watch closely, that as a basic strategy player you were oblivious to. They're all printed out for you in two following tables. These are your real life playing and betting guides for the various games. But remember, *do not exceed a 3 or 4 unit wager in single deck play.* Instead, just top out your bet at a count of "21".

The Complete
KISS COUNT STRATEGY
(for 1 or 2 Decks)

RUNNING COUNT	BETTING STRATEGY	PLAYING STRATEGY	TAKE INSURANCE
off the top thru 19	2 units	Basic	NO
	1 unit	Basic	NO
20	2 units	Advantage	NO
21	4 units	Advantage	Single Deck
22+	*6 units	Advantage	Double Deck

*exceed 3 to 4 units in Double Deck only

148

Now in the shoe games, if the count gets off to a pretty bad start, it's not likely to recover before the shuffle. Consequently, you should walk away from the table if the count has moved soundly in the wrong direction once things have gotten going. Use the discard tray to take your reading, and if your running count is equal to, or lower than the numbers in the following chart, you're done with this shoe.

DECKS	CHECKPOINT	WALK AT
4 Deck Shoe	1 deck played	**"10"** or lower
6 Deck Shoe	1 1/2 dks. played	**"6"** or lower
8 Deck Shoe	2 decks played	**"2"** or lower

These counts will occur on about one shoe in eight. At all other counts, bet and play right on through according to the following chart -- *except* -- *do not exceed 9 units in the four deck games or 10 units with the six deckers.*

The Complete
KISS COUNT STRATEGY
(for 4 to 8 Decks)

RUNNING COUNT	BETTING STRATEGY	PLAYING STRATEGY	TAKE INSURANCE
thru 19	1 unit	Basic	NO
20	3 units	Advantage	NO
21	6 units	Advantage	NO
22	8 units	Advantage	NO
23+	*12 units	Advantage	NO
24+	*12 units	Advantage	NO
25+	*12 units	Advantage	YES

*exceed 9 to 10 units in 8 Deck only

The Bottom Line: So how does the *KISS Count* stack up against the *Ace/10 Front Count* from Chapter 7? The following chart compares the two side by side in a typical six deck game which has the basic strategy player at a $1/2$% disadvantage. It is assumed that $13/4$ decks are cut off at the shuffle:

System	Ace/10 Front Count	KISS Count
Betting	$15-$60-$90	$10-to-$100
Edge	+$1/4$%	+$1/2$%
Avg. Win	$6 per hour	$11 per hour
Median Swing	$270 per hour	$270 per hour
Walkaways	1 shoe in 4	1 shoe in 8
100 hr. Win Rate	55%	60%

The bottom line item in the chart, "100 hour Win Rate" tells you how likely it is that you'll be ahead of the game after 100 hours at the tables -- *providing you play the system perfectly.* As you can see, winning at blackjack is no sure thing. As your hours of playing with an edge mount however, your cumulative chances keep improving. After 1000 hours of playing the *KISS Count,* the chances you'll be a net winner are over 80%. If that still sounds depressing, let me remind you that your chances would be 10% after 1000 hours of perfect basic strategy.

Summary: The *KISS Count* is a condensed, but genuine taste of honest-to-goodness card counting. If you should get good and comfortable with it, improving your game even further is *just a walk in the park.* That's because;

THIS KISS COUNT IS ACTUALLY THE FIRST STAGE OF A THREE STAGE FAMILY OF KISS COUNTS

Once you are easily handling those $61/2$ ranks of cards, upgrading to $81/2$ ranks is as simple as adding one more high card and one more low card to your count. That's called the *Stage II KISS Count.* Using it will increase your $1/2$% edge to nearly $2/3$%. Both the *Stage II* and *Stage III KISS Counts* are presented in Chapter 10.

Chapter 9
KEY POINTS

1) Playing the correct basic strategy will only *minimize* the casino's edge over a player at blackjack. Although Hand Interaction, the "Mag 7" hands and Hi/Lo layout watching will reduce the house edge further, winning with that alone would still be an unlikely proposition.

2) In order to actually gain the upper hand, the player *must* learn to keep track of at least a few *key* ranks of cards.

3) Continuous card counting requires more concentration than a single checkpoint strategy like the Ace/10 Front Count, but it improves your accuracy as the cards play further out.

4) Most full-fledged counting systems track about 80% of the cards. Their sheer mass keeps most blackjack buffs from learning to count.

5) The *KISS Count* is a greatly simplified, *entry level* counting system that will give the player about 2/3 the net edge of a full scale card count .

6) The *KISS Count* not only tells you when to bet more money, but also when to play some hands differently from the basic strategy.

7) There are also situations where your *KISS Count* will point out that it is to your advantage to take Insurance.

8) Playing the *KISS Count* accurately can convert a basic strategy player from a 1/2% underdog to a 1/2% favorite in a typical shoe game.

151

10

the *Stage II & Stage III KISS Counts*

The *KISS Count* from chapter 9 is a *beginner level* introduction to the basic concepts of real card counting. It will groom you to think and play along the same lines as a professional card counter.

For many of you, that will be more than enough to keep you busy. But after a while, if you find yourself comfortable with juggling the numbers in your head, you may want to do a better job of analyzing the condition of the unplayed cards. The good news here is that the *KISS Count* is *"expandable."* As mentioned at the end of Chapter 9, it's merely the *first stage* of an entire family of *KISS* counts.

If and when you feel ready to step up to *"intermediate card counting"*, the *Stage II Kiss Count* should be a simple and logical transition for you. It carries an **89%** rating for betting correlation as opposed to **79%** for its forerunner. In computer simulation runs involving 800 million hands, the *Stage II* count outperformed the original *KISS Count* by roughly an additional $1/6\%$, yielding a net edge of nearly $2/3\%$ in a typical six deck *game (using the same 1-to-10 betting spread)*.

Mind you, these are results achieved by a computer that never miscounts a card, never misplays a hand and never absorbs the cost of tipping a dealer. Also, the computer was never subjected to a range of countermeasures that any casino is likely to impose upon a suspected counter, particularly in 1 and 2 deck games. Nevertheless, with the *Stage II Kiss Count you have an advantage which approaches that of a full scale card count.* Here's how easy it is to convert your original *KISS Count* into the *Stage II Count.*

According to computer studies, the four most important *low* cards in the game of blackjack are the *3, 4, 5* and *6.* So all you do is add the *3* to your count as a "+1" card on the low side -- and add the *10-spot* as a "-1" card on the high side. The following graphic lays out the *Stage II* version in visual form:

the Stage II Kiss Count

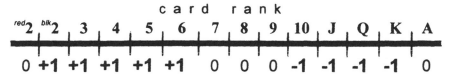

Is that straightforward enough for you? Now you'll be tracking $8^{1}/_{2}$ ranks of cards rather than $6^{1}/_{2}$ and your earning potential will increase by around 30%. You should still practice counting in exactly the same way, and you still need to be able to count down a single deck of cards in 30 seconds. But because the *Stage II Count* tracks more cards, your running count will jump around a little more. As a result, *you'll need to initiate your starting count one point lower* than with the basic *KISS Count* in the shoe games. More specifically;

in **single** deck play;	begin at "18"
in **double** deck play;	begin at "17"
with **four** decks;	begin at "13"
with a **six** deck shoe;	begin at "9"
with **eight** decks;	begin at "5"

This adjustment will get a count of "20" to be worth about the same thing to you in terms of advantage. Therefore, it will still be proper to begin increasing your bets when your running count reaches that same magic number of **"20"**. The following chart outlines a complete and realistic guide for betting your chips with the *Stage II Kiss Count:*

BETTING STRATEGY for the STAGE II KISS COUNT

RUNNING COUNT	SINGLE DECK	DOUBLE DECK	4 DECKS	6 DECKS	8 DECKS
off the top	2u	2u	2u	1 - 2u	1 - 2u
thru 19	1u	1u	1u	1u	1u
20	2u	2u	3u	3u	3u
21	4u	4u	6u	6u	6u
22	4u	6u	9u	9u	9u
23+	4u	6u	9u	10u	12u

Since all running counts away from the norm will occur more often with the *Stage II Count*, your *"Walkaway"* numbers should be a little more extreme. Even so, you'll still be leaving the table due to a bad count just about as often as before. Again, using the discard tray as your reference, walk away if your running count is equal to, or lower than the numbers in the following chart.

DECKS	CHECKPOINT	WALK AT
4 Deck Shoe	1 deck played	**"8"** or lower
6 Deck Shoe	1$\frac{1}{2}$ dks. played	**"4"** or lower
8 Deck Shoe	2 decks played	**"0"** or lower

ADVANTAGE PLAYING STRATEGY for the STAGE II KISS COUNT

Now when it comes to using the *Advantage Playing Strategy*, the *Stage II Kiss Count* is quite a bit more sophisticated. Instead of having just seven custom hands to play *(including Insurance)*, there are *twenty-two!* Not only that, but some plays will kick in at a running count of **"15"**, some at **"20"** and some at

"25" or more. The following two charts will tell you when to deviate from the basic strategy with those twenty-two hands.

ADVANTAGE STRATEGY INDEX NUMBERS
(for 1 & 2 decks) DOUBLE STAND SPLIT

DEALER'S UP-CARD

HAND	2	3	4	5	6	7	9	10	A
8				23	21				
9	19					23			
10								25	24
11									20
12	23	21	18		16				
13	16								
15								24	
16							25	19	
A/7	19								
A/8				23	19	19			
10/10				25	25				

take Insurance @"21" w/sgl. Dk. & @ "23" w/dbl. dk.

ADVANTAGE STRATEGY INDEX NUMBERS
(for 4 to 8 decks) DOUBLE STAND SPLIT

DEALER'S UP-CARD

HAND	2	3	4	5	6	7	9	10	A
8				25	21				
9	19					25			
10								30	28
11									20
12	25	21	a		b				
13	c								
15								27	
16							30	15	
A/7	19								
A/8				25	19	19			
10/10				29	29				

take Insurance @ "25" or higher

a - stand @ **'14'** w/ 4 dks, @ **'11'** w/ 6 dks, and @ **'7'** w/ 8 dks.
b - stand @ **'10'** w/ 4 dks, @ **'5'** w/ 6 dks, and @ **'0'** w/ 8 dks.
c - stand @ **'12'** w/ 4 dks, @ **'7'** w/ 6 dks, and @ **'2'** w/ 8 dks.

155

NOTICE: The bottom line item in each of the two index charts tells you when it becomes mathematically advantageous to split a pair of 10's -- but be careful here! Splitting 10's will almost always be resented by the other players at your table as a total "bonehead" play. Your floorperson however, may become suspicious if he's seen you play a solid game up to now and you suddenly split two 10's with a huge bet up. This play is a double edged sword. On the positive side it will often drive players away from your table and leave the rest of the positive shoe all to you -- as well as yield a percentage edge on the split itself. On the negative side, the floorperson may finger you as a card counter. Although splitting 10's carries a definite advantage when the count is right, you need to feel pretty darn confident about your "welcome mat" in order to do it.

To play your hands by the index numbers on the preceding page, just use the following common blackjack logic;

◆ For "Hit or Stand" hands, *hit* if your running count is *below* the index no. -- *stand* if your count is *equal to* or *above* the index no.
◆ For "Hit or Double" hands, *hit* if your running count is *below* the index no. -- *double* if it is *equal to* or *above* the index no.
◆ For "Stand or Double" hands, *stand* if your running count is *below* the index no. -- *double* if it is *equal to* or *above* the index.
◆ For "Stand or Split" hands, *stand* if your running count is *below* the index no. -- *split* if it is *equal to* or *above* the index.
◆ For any blank squares -- *always play by basic strategy.*

Just to be sure you've got it straight, let's look at the following illustration. It's a six deck shoe and we'll say that you're playing all three hands. Your running count is **"25"**.

The dealer has a *6* up and your first hand is *8*. The index number for doubling with *8* against a *6* is '**21**'. Since your running count equals or exceeds that number, doubling down is the correct play.

Your second hand is *12*. The index number for standing is '**5**' *(from the footnotes beneath the chart),* and since your running count is at or above that, you must stand.

Your third hand is a *soft 19*. The index number for doubling is '**19**', and since your count is at or beyond that, doubling is the play *(note that if the dealer happened to have an Ace up rather than a 6, you'd insure all three hands because a '25' count warrants Insurance).*

Now, what if you had those same three hands against that *6* up with a count of say, only '**4**'? Since that's below all three index numbers, you'd just hit the *8* and the *12,* then stand on the *soft 19.*

IF THE DEALER HITS SOFT 17

The index charts on page 155 assume the dealer *stands* on *soft 17*. If the dealer *hits soft 17*, a few hands will be affected. This typically applies when the dealer has an *Ace* or a *6* up and is liable to turn over a *soft 17*. With *stand soft 17* the hand would now be over. But with *hit soft 17*, she could still improve or even bust. Hence, revised index numbers for *hit soft 17 (H17)* are given below.

(for 1 & 2 DECKS)

	UP-CARD	
HAND	6	A
11		17
12	14	
16		24
A/8	17	

(for 4 to 8 DECKS)

	UP-CARD	
HAND	6	A
11		12
12	std	
16		27
A/8	13	

(Note that not making these index adjustments will lower your net edge about .01%)

PLAYING SURRENDER

With basic strategy, 4 hands should be surrendered in a typical shoe game. But with the *KISS Count*, you should surrender between 0 and 8 hands *(between 0 and 11 hands if H17)* based on the running count. The table on page 158 tells you when to surrender if it's allowed. If your running count equals or exceeds the index number, then *surrender*. If it's lower, just *hit (except as noted).*

157

KISS SURRENDER CHART

DOUBLE DECK SURRENDER @

	9	10	A^S17	A^H17
14		23		23
15	21	18	19	17
16	18	15	16	14
17			(12)	(19)
8/8		20		(17)

SHOE GAME SURRENDER @

	9	10	A^S17	A^H17
14		25		25
15	21	12	19	13
16	12	0	5	-5
17				(19)
8/8		20		(16)

*(xx) – Play in reverse: Surrender if the running count is this or **LESS***

PLAYER'S EV at "EVEN" & POSITIVE COUNTS

The EV table compares your average gain/loss *(expected value)* with each index play when the running count is **'even'** vs. when it's **'29'**. It illustrates why you should deviate from basic strategy when the count reaches a given level. Figures are expressed as a percentage of the initial bet.

PLAYER'S HAND	at 'EVEN' COUNT HIT	at 'EVEN' COUNT DOUBLE	'29' RUNNING COUNT HIT	'29' RUNNING COUNT DOUBLE
8 vs. 5	+8%	+3%	+15%	+18%
8 vs. 6	+12%/+11%	+10%/+9%	+19%/+17%	+24%/+22%
9 vs. 2	+8%	+7%	+13%	+20%
9 vs. 7	+18%	+12%	+22%	+26%
10 vs. 10	+3%	0%	+4%	+6%
10 vs. A	+8%/+3%	-1%/-3%	+13%/+9%	+17%/+15%
11 vs. A	+15%/+11%	+13%/+12%	+19%/+16%	+28%

PLAYER'S HAND	HIT	STAND	HIT	STAND
12 vs. 2	-25%	-29%	-27%	-24%
12 vs. 3	-23%	-25%	-24%	-19%
12 vs. 4	-21%	-21%	-21%	-13%
12 vs. 6	-17%	-15%/-12%	-18%	-9%/-6%
13 vs. 2	-31%	-30%	-33%	-24%
15 vs. 10	-50$\frac{1}{2}$%	-54%	-57%	-56%
16 vs. 9	-50$\frac{1}{2}$%	-54%	-55%	-56%
16 vs. 10	-53$\frac{1}{2}$%	-54%	-59%	-56%

PLAYER'S HAND	STAND	DOUBLE	STAND	DOUBLE
A/7 vs. 2	+12%	+12%	+15%	+20%
A/8 vs. 4	+42%	+35%	+45%	+49%
A/8 vs. 5	+44%	+41%	+48%	+55%
A/8 vs. 6	+49%/+45%	+48%/+46%	+53%/49%	+61%/+59%

PLAYER'S HAND	STAND	SPLIT	STAND	SPLIT
10/10 vs. 5	+67%	+51%	+69%	+76% w/rspl
10/10 vs. 6	+70%/+68%	+57%/+56%	+72%/+70%	+82% w/rspl

	TAKE	DECLINE	TAKE	DECLINE
INSURANCE	-7%	0%	+4%	0%

Now, for tracking two extra card ranks and memorizing 21 index numbers, how much will the *Stage II Kiss* improve your game over the original *KISS Count?* A performance comparison for a typical six deck game with 1³/4 decks cut off is shown below:

System	KISS Count	Stage II Kiss
Betting	$10-to-$100	$10-to-$100
Net Edge	**+.48%**	**+.64%**
Avg. Win	$11 per hour	$14.⁵⁰ per hour
Median Swing	$270 per hour	$270 per hour
Walkaways	1 shoe in 8	1 shoe in 8
100 hr. Win Rate	60%	63%

If 21 index numbers seem like too much work, you could play the *Stage II Count* with the original *KISS* hand strategy on page 146. That'll reduce the *Kiss II* yields to about +.58% and $13.25 per hour.

Well, that's the *Stage II Kiss Count*. It gives lots of performance bang for being as basic as it is. But if you still crave more horsepower, then your next system upgrade is just a paragraph away.

the STAGE III KISS COUNT

The further you move up the ladder with blackjack counting systems, the less additional gain the same amount of extra work yields. The *Stage II Kiss Count* is a good enough system to use for the rest of your life if you want. No matter how complex you get with your count, you'll never be able to increase your earning potential more than about another 20% beyond that.

However, if you've been handling the *Stage II* count with room to spare, there's another step you can take using the same unbalanced "KISS" format. Just include the 7 in your card count as a "+1" on the low side along with the *Ace* as a "-1" on the high side. That upgrade gives you the *Stage III Kiss Count* which carries a formidable **96%** rating for betting correlation. It'll improve your net edge by about another ¹/16% over the *Stage II* count, yielding a ⁷/10% overall advantage in the typical six deck game with the same 1-to-10 betting spread and a 1³/4 deck cutoff.

**THIS PERFORMANCE IS ON PAR WITH THE OTHER
TWO MOST POPULAR COUNT SYSTEMS IN USE TODAY**

159

Those would be the *Hi/Lo* and *KO* counts. Yet with its streamlined formatting, the *Stage III Kiss* ought to be simpler to learn and use. A graphic of the *Stage III Kiss Count* is shown below:

the **Stage III Kiss Count**

c a r d   r a n k

^{red}2	^{blk}2	3	4	5	6	7	8	9	10	J	Q	K	A
0	+1	+1	+1	+1	+1	+1	0	0	-1	-1	-1	-1	-1

The *Stage III KISS Count* yields 85 to 90% of all that it's possible to gain with some of the most complex professional count systems that exist today. When using it, **simply initiate your running count at all the same starting points as the Stage II Count -- no adjustment is needed.** You'll still increase your bets when the running count reaches **"20"**, but again, these counts will be uncovered even a little more often. When practicing, you'll find that counting down a single deck in 30 seconds will be an even greater challenge, but it remains a staunch requirement.

Also, due to the improved structural precision resulting in more frequent high counts, your betting schedule will be slightly *stretched out* to keep your volatility the same. The next chart outlines a complete betting guide for the *Stage III Kiss Count:*

BETTING STRATEGY for the
STAGE III KISS COUNT

RUNNING COUNT	SINGLE DECK	DOUBLE DECK	4 DECKS	6 DECKS	8 DECKS
off the top	2u	2u	2u	1 - 2u	1 - 2u
thru 19	1u	1u	1u	1u	1u
20	2u	2u	3u	3u	3u
21	3u	3u	5u	5u	5u
22	4u	5u	8u	8u	8u
23+	4u	6u	9u	10u	12u

Index Numbers & Walk Points: Just use all the same index numbers for the *Stage III Kiss* as for *Kiss II (from pages 155, 157 & 158)*. You can also follow the same "walkaway" numbers in the shoe games *(from page 154)*.

OVERALL ADVANTAGE AS THE COUNT RISES

Below is your overall advantage at various KISS III running counts, and how often each count (or higher) will occur in six deck play with 4¹/₄ decks dealt out.

Running Count	"14"	"17"	"20"	"23"	"26"	"29"	"32"
ADVANTAGE	-.4%	0%	+.5%	+1.0%	+1.6%	+2.3%	+3.0%
Occurrence	*45%*	*29%*	*19%*	*10%*	*6%*	*2%*	*1%*

Performance Summary: All three *KISS Counts* are easier to use than most count systems out there today. *But how do they perform?* The chart below summarizes a 1.5 billion hand computer simulation, comparing each *KISS Count* to the *Hi/Lo* and *KO* Counts. All are unbalanced counts except *Hi/Lo,* which is balanced and requires true count conversion. All played the same six deck game with a 0.48% basic strategy house edge. Each system played 300 million hands. All used a 1-to-10 bet spread and had the same size average wager. All shuffles came with 1³/₄ decks remaining.

Count System	KISS Count	Stage II Kiss	Stage III Kiss	KO Count	Hi/Lo Count
Betting	$10-$100	$10-$100	$10-$100	$10-$100	$10-$100
Avg. Bet	$21	$21	$21	$21	$21
Median Swing	$270/hr	$270/hr	$270/hr	$270/hr	$270/hr
Avg. Win	$11/hr	$14.⁵⁰/hr	$16/hr	$15.⁵⁰/hr	$16.⁵⁰/hr
Net Edge	**+.48%**	**+.64%**	**+.70%**	**+.68%**	**+.72%**
Walkaways	1 in 8	1 in 8	1 in 8	1 in 8	1 in 8
100 hr win rate	60%	63%	65%	64%	65%

*Note: KISS yields reflect counting half the deuces as +1; **not** all deuces as +¹/₂. KO used 21 individual indices rather than the simpler KO Preferred. Hi/Lo used 75 "true count" indices, since balanced systems deviate from basic strategy more accurately at negative and extremely positive counts. The chart on page 194 compares these yields against several other more sophisticated systems.*

The *KISS III* is about as sophisticated as you'd care to get with single level unbalanced card counting. It combines rock solid performance with ease of use, making it a logical/practical choice for the mainstream card counter. But no matter what count you may use, you still must digest Chapter 11, *the Art & Science of Skillful Play.* It outlines several tactical skills and "image" traits needed to play unimpeded by the casino pit. Some optional tune-ups that can improve the *KISS III* yield beyond that of the *Hi/Lo* are also given.

Chapter 10
KEY POINTS

1) The *Stage II* and *Stage III Kiss Counts* are natural progressive extensions of the original *KISS Count*. You can "grow" into them by simply adding one extra low and one extra high card at a time to your basic *KISS Count* structure.

2) Used accurately, the *Stage II Kiss Count* will gain about an additional .15% edge over the basic *KISS Count* in a typical six deck game.

3) The *Stage III* Count will then gain about another .06% over the *Stage II* Count in that same game.

4) Both the *Stage II* and *Stage III* Counts use 22 *count activated* custom hand plays (including Insurance), rather than just the 7 basic plays supplied with the basic *KISS Count*.

5) Sticking with 7 basic custom hand plays rather than using all 22 will decrease the *Stage II* and *Stage III* performances by about .06% in a shoe game.

6) Also, learning to use all 22 custom hand plays with the basic *KISS Count* will improve its own performance by about .06% as well.

7) The *Stage III Kiss Count* performs on a par with the other popular single level counts, but its streamlined format is more user friendly.

11

the Art and Science of Skillful Play

With the proper playing strategy and a reasonably capable count system such as any of the *Kiss Counts*, you are *mathematically* equipped to beat the game of blackjack. But "mathematically" is a big word here. You see, winning at casino *"21"* is a two step process. First you must learn the **science** of how to beat the game. Then you have to learn the **art** of how to beat the house.

The *first* part is no piece of cake. Most players who try, never really quite get the hang of counting cards. The *Kiss Counts* should make that part considerably easier for you. But it's still that *second* step which stops all but the very most dedicated and diligent blackjack buffs from beating the game -- long term! Right now would be a good time to remind you that;

SUCCEEDING AT BLACKJACK WILL REQUIRE NO LESS EFFORT AND FORTITUDE THAN BECOMING A "90" GOLFER, OR A "175" BOWLER

For some that'll come easy, and for others it'll be very tough. *(note that in the original issue of this book, succeeding at blackjack was*

163

*equated to golfing "par" or bowling 200. I've come to believe that was an overstatement **then** -- and certainly is **now** with the advent of the Ace/10 Front Count and the basic KISS Count).*

Still though, it's one thing to understand what makes blackjack tick and set your mind to mastering a winning count system. That's the *scientific* part. You can learn a lot of scientific things from books. But if counting cards is all you ever learn, you've only armed yourself with enough knowledge to land in a world of trouble! That's because, ***all the technical studying in the world won't teach you the art of how to be the mouse that sneaks the cheese out from under the cat's nose without his realizing you were capable of taking it!*** That only comes with perseverance and seasoning. A successful blackjack player has to be part *scholar* and part *street hustler*. Just knowing a winning count system is not enough!

Once you become thoroughly proficient at counting cards and playing your hands correctly, there are several other tangible skills that must also become an integral part of your blackjack repertoire. Most of them are described in this chapter.

PLAYABLE RULES

First and foremost, not all blackjack games are beatable, although most of them are. The biggest initial basic strategy disadvantage you can probably afford to start out with would be about 0.75%. Use the *"Rule Variations"* table from Chapter 5 in this book to evaluate each particular game available to you.

Recognize however, that some rules affect the card counter more than the basic strategy player and vise-versa. The surrender option for example, is more valuable to a card counter due to his increased likelihood of being dealt *15* or *16* against a *10* up when he has a big bet out there. That's because these hand scenarios are often comprised of two *10's* and only one *non-10*. Plus, most fully structured count systems will tell the counter when it's proper to surrender some other hands such as *14* against

164

a *10*, or *15* vs. a *9*. Such opportunities arise only when the player has a large bet up. *Surrender is a BIG asset to the card counter,* yielding an extra 0.20% to 0.25% in multi-deck play. It also lowers your volatility by smoothing out the "bumps". As a result, you can bet a little higher while running the same risk of ruin. Just exactly how much bigger you can bet depends upon whether you bring your *daily* stake, your *trip* stake or your *entire bankroll* into the picture.

A) If the casino you're at today happens to offer surrender, you can bet 4% higher with the same chance of losing your one day pocket stake.

B) If you're on vacation with a five day trip stake and play surrender the whole time, betting 7% bigger gives you the same chance of blowing that trip stake.

C) If you *never, ever* play anything but surrender, you can bet 20% bigger on the same total bankroll. Together with surrender's higher percentage edge, a "would be" $25 per hour expected win rate becomes:

$34 per hour on a 4 hour **daily stake**
$35 per hour on a 25 hour **trip stake**
$39 per hour on a 500 hour **bankroll**

Single Deck 6-5 Blackjack: Single deck games which pay

only 6-to-5 on blackjack rather than the full 3-to-2 add 1.39% to the basic house edge *(see page 82)*. At crowded tables, you need a 1-to-10 betting spread with a decent count system just to break even. Heads up, you need 1-to-6. Leave these games to the tourists.

Beware the CSM: "Continuous shuffling machines" are a

different animal than "automatic shufflers". At an eight deck table, an auto-shuffler simply shuffles one eight deck setup of cards while the dealer deals another. When the shuffle comes, the dealer puts the original eight deck pack into the shuffler, then drops the freshly shuffled pack into the shoe. It simply saves down time *(and thwarts shuffle trackers)*, but changes nothing else.

Now with *continuous shufflers* the cards are dealt from a mechanical shoe that is constantly interleaving all the cards inside it. At the end of each round, the dealer inserts the discards into a slot at the rear of the shuffler, and those cards are then interleaved with those mixing inside. Although there might be some "latency", or delay in getting the just used cards mixed with the others, very few cards if any can be counted as having been eliminated. Thus, your opportunity to extract an edge has been in effect, *destroyed!*

165

DECK PENETRATION

This is a huge factor in obtaining an edge for the card counter. The term "deck penetration" defines how far the deck is dealt out before the shuffle occurs. As we progress into the 21st century, deck penetration seems to be growing worse and worse. With a six deck shoe, it's become pretty typical to cut off the last 1³/4 decks -- plus or minus ¹/4 deck. Eight deck shoes usually cut off the last two decks.

Now, a 1¹/2 deck cutoff in a six deck game is quite a bit better than a 2 deck chop. It's pretty important to go where they deal out more cards -- all else being equal. Even within the same casino, you can often find dealers who give a more favorable cutoff than others. On rare occasion in a few choice places, they might even cut off only the last deck! That would be a dream situation. Conversely, anything worse than a 2 deck chop in a six deck game is a "gouge", and not worthy of your action. With eight decks you might be able to tolerate a 2¹/4 deck chop -- *max*.

To give you an idea of just how much difference good and bad penetration can make, three separate 100 million hand simulations were run using the *Mentor Count (an advanced card count which follows in the next chapter)*. The conditions were; **six decks; stand on soft 17; double on any two cards including after splits; no re-splitting of any pairs**. The betting spread was 1-to-10. The basic strategy player was at a disadvantage of 0.48%. *The only variable in the simulations were the shuffle points*. I started with a two deck cut-off, and after 100 million hands changed to a 1¹/2 deck shuffle point, then finally to a one deck cutoff. The results for each 100 million hands, are listed below:

CUTOFF POINT	PLAYER RESULT
2 DECKS	+0.65%
1¹/2 DECKS	+0.90%
1 DECK	+1.15%

As you can see, even with a powerful tool like the *Mentor Count,* a two deck cutoff hurts you badly in a six deck game! To play

166

against the shoes with bad "pen", you need to have an awful lot of other good things going in the way of rules, betting spread, etc!

Some Redeeming Value: *Although poor penetration is never a good thing, the figures in the previous chart are not the total "bottom line" in the penetration issue. That's because most of your really high counts will come near the end of the shoe. But if they've cut off 2 decks out of six, many of your "would be" 10 unit bets will just get shuffled away. The other side of that coin is, **your volatility will also be reduced.** If you're adequately bankrolled to tolerate the swings that a 1 1/2 deck cutoff will dump on you -- **then a 2 deck cutoff will reduce those swings by 8%!** That is, you'll have a lower standard deviation. This will allow you to increase your betting action and still face the same original risk to the same bankroll.*

*There's a "right" way to go about doing this. If you merely raised all your bets by 8%, you'd have the same standard deviation, or volatility as with the smaller bets and the better penetration. But more ground than that can actually be made up by keeping the same size min. and max. bets **while steepening your betting ramp!***

If you would've reached your 10 unit bet at +3 true, bet 10 units at +2 1/2 true when you've got lousy penetration. If you were doing 4 units at +2 true, do 5 units there. It's okay, because your averaged bet size would've been cut down considerably otherwise. So just speed up your betting ramp by about 25% and you'll have the same volatility as before. That'll get back about 25% of the dollars that went out the window when you lost your penetration.

Now in double deck play, some dealers are nice enough to deal out the first 2/3 of the pack *(leaving only 35 undealt cards)*. That would be excellent! But in many houses they may insert the cut card midway through the pack, cutting off the second full deck. Those are the games you want to avoid. A minimally acceptable cutoff for double deck play is when the cut card is placed about 45 cards from the bottom -- giving you the first 60 cards or so to play with.

Deck penetration in single deck play is very dependent upon how crowded the tables are. It will be virtually impossible to get adequate penetration at a jammed up table. *Playing with one deck, you absolutely must get a third hand in before the shuffle!* Let that be your barometer. This will seldom occur with more than three players in action.

167

NUMBER of PLAYERS

Playing at a full table is undesirable to the card counter for two reasons. The most important one is, since you theoretically have an edge you won't be implementing that edge unless you're playing! At a full table you spend a lot of time watching other people play blackjack. The speed at which the hands are dealt varies *dramatically* with the number of players. How many hands you play in an hour's time also depends upon the speed of each dealer, how many decks are in play and whether automatic shufflers are used. But in general the following chart will be fairly accurate.

PLAYERS AT THE TABLE	HANDS PER HOUR
7	55
6	65
5	75
4	90
3	110
2	150
1	230

If you're heads up *(alone)* with the dealer for fifteen minutes, you can actually get in an hour's worth of "full table" blackjack play! This alone is good cause to avoid crowded tables. But there's another lesser reason why you'd like to be as isolated with the dealer as possible. As a counter, in order to acquire an advantage you need to play against deck compositions that have become skewed *(to the high side)*. This can never happen until some cards are removed from play. The more cards that are removed, the more likely this is to occur and the more skewed the remaining cards will become!

Suppose you were playing double deck blackjack and the dealer consistently placed the plastic cut card 40 cards from the bottom of the pack. At a *full table* you would usually be dealt only *three rounds* before the shuffle. One-third of your bets would be placed against a full pack *(where you always have a disadvantage)*. When you made your first bet, there will have been no cards removed. When you size your bet for the second and third hands, a total of about 22 and 44 cards will have played out, respectively. At the completion of the third hand, the shuffle will come. Each of those three times you placed your bet, the *average* number of cards in the remaining pack was about 82.

But if it were a *three handed* game you would get in *six or seven hands* between shuffles! Only about 15% of your bets will be made off the top of the pack. And across all six or seven hands, an average of about 77 cards will be left in the pack at the time you size each wager. What I'm saying is;

PLAYING IN A SHORTER-HANDED GAME HAS THE EFFECT OF ACQUIRING DEEPER OVERALL DECK PENETRATION!

The difference is not always this significant, but you *do* tend to play against fewer remaining cards at emptier tables! In shoe games, the difference is much less important. That's because proportionally speaking, there's a bigger difference between 77 and 82 cards than there is between 200 and 205 *(about average for six deck play)*.

In the following table, the *Mentor Count* was used to play single deck and six deck blackjack, first heads up *(alone with the dealer)*, and then seven-handed. For the six deck runs, the same rules were in force as with the deck penetration experiment back on page 166 *(-.48% basic strategy)*. The betting spread remained at 1-to-10 and the cut-off point was a typical 1³/4 decks. For single deck, the dealer hit soft *17*, and the player could not double after splits *(-.21% basic strategy)*. The betting spread was 1-to-3 and no hand was dealt with fewer than 22 cards remaining.

DECKS	PLAYERS	RESULT
1	1	+.90%
1	7	+.65%
6	1	+.77%
6	7	+.69%

169

Here you can see that the fewer the decks, the more important it becomes that the table is not crowded. Now consider that heads up, you'll get in four times as many hands per hour and it becomes obvious that the number of players is a serious factor. Once again, *three players is the maximum for hand held blackjack. Four players is tolerable in the shoe games.*

BETTING SPREAD

With blackjack, even an expert player is an underdog in the game the majority of the time. Except for rare cases where the rules are superb and the decks are very few, the card counter only has the advantage when there is a surplus of high cards remaining. During these advantageous periods he basically must put more money in action than he did all the rest of the time in order to become a worthwhile mathematical favorite in the overall game.

Don't think just because you're increasing your bets when the count rises that you automatically have the overall edge. If you're able to use a 1-to-4 betting spread in a typical *single* deck game, yes, you'll have the best of it. That's because the high/low proportion of remaining cards ranges wildly when there were only 52 cards to begin with! Your opportunities to make those three and four unit wagers will arise very frequently. But that same spread just won't get it done with a *312 card shoe!*

The shoe game is slow and dull by card counting standards. That is, you'll be counting and waiting to raise your bets, sometimes for several shoes running. Mathematically, all that time represents lost money because you'll have the short end of the stick pretty much throughout. When a solid positive count finally comes along, you're going to have to get some serious money out there to compensate for the drought. About a 1-to-10 spread is the minimum that would be worthwhile here. If you're not a familiar face in this particular casino, you can probably get away with more for a while. But eventually, you're probably going to have to work with 1-to-10.

170

One good thing about multi-deck shoes is, the count usually rises so gradually that you'll seldom have trouble betting in direct proportion to it. Besides that, pit crews are pretty tolerant of wide betting spreads in shoe games. They're of the opinion that multi-deck games, particularly six or more decks are pretty tough to beat, *and they are right!*

Single and double deck blackjack on the other hand is a much spunkier game. You'll often find your count indicating a single unit bet on one hand, a six unit wager on the next and a single on the hand after that! But *no way* can you get away with changing your bet sizes that abruptly! Pit crews in these games are ever-vigilant for signs of card counters, *and that would be a dead giveaway!*

With one deck, a "2-1-4" betting spread may be about the best you'll be able to use over an extended period of time; perhaps even 2-1-3! That means starting off each new deck with a two unit bet, then either cutting back or increasing on the next hand according to the count. Many times you won't even get to double your bet without causing a shuffle up unless you've won the last hand and have let both bets ride. You'll need good rules if you're forced to keep your betting this flat; probably no worse than -0.3% basic strategy. If you're 20 cards into the deck, have lost your last two unit wager and the count calls for a three or four unit bet on the next hand but you fear the dealer will shuffle, *then just bet another two units!*

YOU POSITIVELY MUST AVOID SHUFFLE UPS!

If you don't, you'll be getting all the negative decks and neutral decks to play with, but not the positive ones. The distribution of cards you'll be playing against will have been artificially altered to favor the house. In effect, *it will be like playing with a deck stripped of some of its high cards!*

At the same time, being pressured into making nearly flat bets is not a good situation either. Single deck play requires more art than any other *"21"* game. Until you're really comfortable playing cat and mouse with the pit crew, you may be better off in the multi-deck games.

171

Two deck *"21"* can be a pretty good game. The count moves quickly enough so that you'll be moving your bets up and down regularly. If you can be smooth about it, a 1-to-6 spread is not that difficult to achieve. Coming off the top of each deck betting two and three units alternately will help you "bury" your 6 unit wagers later on. If you look for a decent cut card placement, have pretty good rules and don't play more than three-handed, those two or three unit bets off the top won't be too big a factor. Be extra careful with *any* hand held game however, because heat from the pit or surveillance room is never far off.

The following table assumes average rules and normal deck penetration. Based upon that, your *minimum* satisfactory betting spread in each type of game is recommended. More is better if you can manage it -- *but don't cut your own throat.*

NUMBER of DECKS	BETTING SPREAD
1	2-1-3
2	1 to 5
4	1 to 8
6	1 to 10
8	1 to 12

TRUE FUDGING

Since unbalanced counts are quite a bit easier to use and lose very little in the way of performance, many new card counters choose the *unbalanced* route over *balanced*. Still, once a player learns his unbalanced count well, he may become concerned over the fact that in most cases, it merely *estimates* his "true count."

When he's got a huge bet riding and has the hand shown on the next page with a high running count, *he may be reluctant to stand as his system might recommend at that point.* He realizes there's a margin of error in playing his hands strictly by the running count, and most of the time that's okay. But right here, right now;

HE WISHES HE HAD MORE EXACT INFORMATION!

If you share that same queasiness about these kinds of hands, *true fudging* can help. Here's how. The *Stage II* and *III Kiss* index charts tell you to stand in a six deck game with *15* against a *10* if the running count is "**27**" or more. But that's just a good *averaged number!* In reality, if you encountered that hand after only two decks had been played out, you shouldn't stand at less than "**29**". Yet, if you're near the shuffle you should stand at "**25**". All three of those running counts at their respective penetration levels will equal a true count *("count per deck")* of **+4** -- which is the *real* number at which you should stand. But if you want to play that hand strictly by the running count, "**27**" is your best number.

This error margin exists to one degree or another at all running counts -- *except* "**21**", where it is always exactly "**+2 true**". The closer to "**21**" you are, the less possible error there is.

An example of a hand with minimal playing error would be *9* against a *deuce*. There, the *Kiss* index charts tell you to double down at a running count of "**19**" or higher. The actual count at which you want to make this play is "**+1 true**". Well, in a six deck game, a running count of "**19**" after two decks have been played equals a true count of "**+1.5**". Near the shuffle where maybe only 1 3/4 decks are left, that running count of "**19**" equals "**+0.9 true**". So as finicky as you might be about your accuracy, any running

173

counts between '**19**' and '**23**' remain accurate enough that they're just not worth worrying about. But at '**24**' and above where there's more error, you can regain most of your lost accuracy by:

KNOWING HOW TO *FUDGE* YOUR INDEX NUMBERS

The following chart shows the error margin between your running count and the "true count" depending upon how deep you are into a six deck shoe.

RUNNING COUNT	TRUE COUNT with "x" DECKS DEALT OUT				
	1 dk	2 dks	3 dks	4 dks	4.5 dks
"17"	+1.2	+1.0	+0.7	0	-0.7
"19"	+1.6	+1.5	+1.3	+1.0	+0.7
"21"	+2.0	+2.0	+2.0	+2.0	+2.0
"23"	+2.4	+2.5	+2.7	+3.0	+3.3
"25"	+2.8	+3.0	+3.3	+4.0	+4.7
"27"	N/A	+3.5	+4.0	+5.0	+6.0
"29"	N/A	N/A	+4.7	+6.0	+7.3

You can correct for this error in both shoe and double deck games by routinely "fudging" your index numbers as described below.

◆ Index numbers from '**24**' to '**26**' need to be *one point higher* if it's early in the deal -- & *one point lower* when near the shuffle.

◆ Index nos. of '**27**' and above get shaded *two points upward* if it's very early, only *one point upward* if it's just rather early, --- then *one point downward* if it's getting moderately late, and *two points downward* as you approach the shuffle.

◆ In the heart of the deck/shoe, use the given index number as is.

This *fudging* principle also applies to Insurance and bet sizing in shoe games. Since you'd normally insure at '**25**', you'll need '**26**' if it's early in the shoe and only '**24**' approaching the shuffle, etc.

FUDGING IN THIS WAY IS PRACTICALLY AS ACCURATE AS TRUE COUNT CONVERTING A BALANCED COUNT

after all the residue has settled from a balanced player's *estimation* of the discard tray and *rounding off* his multiplication or division.

Now, *low running counts* get trickier. That's because unbalanced systems are calibrated in the direction of rising counts. At low counts, the link between the running count and the true count basically dissolves. It's *not* a serious flaw, since you'll be betting the minimum – or will have already deserted the table. Still, if you wish to play your hands more accurately at low counts, there's a way

174

to do it. Take a look at the two hands below:

HAND "A"   HAND "B"

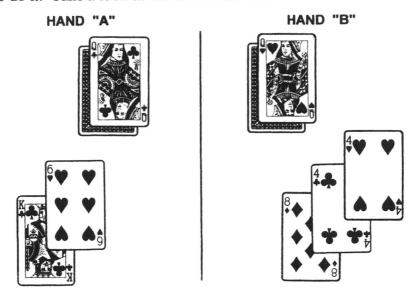

Let's say you're playing the *Stage III Kiss Count*, and on your first hand off the top of a six deck shoe you're dealt hand "A". Your index chart says to stand with *16* against a *10* if your count is **"15"** or higher. Having started off at **"9"**, you now have a running count of **"8"** so you hit. No problem.

But what if you had hand "B" instead? This time your running count would be **"10"**, again dictating that you hit. But we already know from earlier in this book that off the top with these cards, you should stand. ***There's the problem!*** Once again, that index number of **"15"** merely serves as an all around compromise. In fact, if you were 4 1/2 decks into that six deck shoe, it would actually be best to hit all the way through **"18"**! So what's the answer? Technically speaking, you should play both hands like this:

REMAINING DECKS	STAND AT
6	"10"
5	"12"
4	"14"
3	"16"
2	"18"
1 1/2	"19"

175

2017 UPDATE

Why? Because in reality, you should **stand** with any kind of *16* against a *10* if the count is the least bit *higher* than *"normal"*, even if by only one card. And since the *KISS Count* tracks two more low cards than high cards, the count will naturally drift upward by two points per dealt deck, as shown below.

DISCARD TRAY CONTAINS	NORMAL COUNT IS
0 decks	'9'
1 deck	'11'
2 decks	'13'
3 decks	'15'
4 decks	'17'
4½ decks	'18'

When the running count matches these shoe levels, the *high card/ low card* balance of the shoe will be *'even'*. As you play and the discard tray fills, be aware of what count would be *even* for each level. If a low count hand arises and your running count is *below even* by *at least* the number in the following table, just *hit** that hand! Doing this will link your running count closer to the true count and be more accurate than going by one fixed index number.

SIMPLY **HIT** IF YOUR RUNNING COUNT IS BELOW 'EVEN'
BY *(at least)* THE NUMBER OF CARDS SHOWN BELOW

Your Hand	2	3	4	5	6^{S17}	6^{H17}	10	A^{H17}
9		-4						
11								-4
12			-1	-7	-4	std		
13	-5							
16							0	
A/2				-2				
A/4			-2					
A/8*						-3 std		

DEALER'S UP-CARD

The first hand in the chart is 9 against a 3. Suppose there are two decks in the discard tray where a count of '13' would be even. If it's '9' or lower at this shoe level, just HIT 9 vs.3. Later, when there are four decks in the tray, just HIT this hand if the count is '13' or lower.

SUMMARY: So how much is low count *fudging* worth? Not nearly as much as at high counts because of the smaller bet size at stake. But when you've got a close hand at a mediocre to poor count and you're hesitating, the above chart will tell you with improved accuracy when it's time to deviate from basic strategy.

HALF POINT COUNTING

All the *Kiss Counts* require you to track just half the *deuces* in the deck. Arnold Snyder's *Red 7 Count* and the *Black Ace Counts* from the original edition of this book also ignore half of a particular card rank. As weird as that may seem, it's an excellent mechanism for connecting the running count to the true count. When Snyder first came up with the idea in the early '80's, it was a stroke of genius. Ignoring half a card rank and counting the other half however, does leave the door open to one more possible small performance enhancement. That would be to;

**COUNT *ALL* THE CARDS OF THE
DIVIDED RANK AS ½ POINT**

rather than *half* of them as 1 full point. The *Kiss Count* for example would then count *all* the *deuces* as +½ point. It's a tad more accurate than counting just half of them as +1 since the *deuce* is a less significant card to begin with *and* -- you'd be monitoring the dispersion of more cards. So then starting off at **"9"** in a six deck game, if the first six cards to come out were;

your running count would be **"9½"**. It won't fall back onto a whole number until another *deuce* comes out. Everything else gets played in exactly the same way. To simplify reciting these half numbers in your head, just say, *"9a"*, rather than *"9-and-a-half"*. When a *deuce* comes next, you'd go from *"9a"* to *"10"*, etc.

If you're playing low stakes, half point counting will be more of a headache than it's worth. To its credit, it improves the betting correlation of *Stage II Kiss* to **90%**, and *Stage III Kiss* to **97%**.

But what can that mean in dollars? Extensive computer runs indicate that you'll pick up around .02%. So you need to spread $20-to-$200 to gain an extra $1 an hour from it in a shoe game.

TABLE HOPPING

Another method of getting more money down as the favorite and less when the your a "dog" is leaving the table when the count goes substantially negative. This tactic applies mostly to shoe games since there, positive and negative counts tend to last a good while.

An extension of this same principle is to approach a blackjack game at the beginning of the shoe and count down the first few hands from the aisle. This is known as *"backcounting"*. If the count climbs significantly into the "plus", jump in and play a bit. If not, move on towards the next table with the same game plan in mind. This technique is nothing new and;

SHOULD BE AN INTEGRAL PART OF
YOUR GAME IF YOU PLAY THE SHOES

Backcounting has also been coined as "Wonging" in card counting jargon *(named after Stanford Wong and his landmark book "Professional Blackjack")*. As a matter of general practice in shoe games, you should make it a point to quit for the day or go to the bathroom on a negative count rather than at the end of a shoe. The same goes for changing tables or breaking to eat. You need to do whatever you can to minimize your percentage of time in action as the underdog. Once you've gone through the first 70 or 80 cards of a shoe and have a low count, why absorb the ensuing cluster of disadvantageous deals?

Backcounting Under the Radar: When backcounting, you should *not* camp out directly behind a table, focusing on the cards every moment. Wait until all the initial two card hands have been dealt, then move in, scan the board and get your count. Hang around while the hands are played, then walk partly away the moment all the cards for that round have been exposed. You'll have 10 or 15 seconds to be out of sight while the dealer settles all bets, scoops up the cards and deals out the next round. That's when you need to get the cards back in your sights. You can usually do this from a distance of 10 or even 15 feet, by;

"PIPWATCHING"

Do *not* try to read the index number on each card. Instead,

178

become familiar with the *pip arrangement* of each card value. It's easy to tell a *5*, from a *2*, from a *10* just by recognizing the pip arrangement. The toughest two cards to distinguish between from a distance are the *8-spot* and the *10-spot* because of their similar pip arrangements. All the rest are a piece of cake.

As for backing *out* of shoes with low counts? Understand that if you play the *Kiss Count,* you're monitoring more low cards than high ones. As a result, anytime your running count is not *rising,* then more actual high cards have come out than low ones and your disadvantage has actually increased! With *Kiss,* it's easy enough to simply pick a relatively early checkpoint in the shoe and have a pre-set count at which you'll jump ship.

The *Mentor Count (from Chapter 12)* is a more precisioned animal. With *Mentor,* you're constantly updating the true count all along the way? Since you always have that information, simply leave *anytime* the *true count* descends to a particular level.

The table hopping guidelines below can help skew the overall distribution of cards you'll face somewhat more in your favor. Following them will help your bottom line.

1) **Start off each playing session on a positive count via back-counting** (enter @ "20" w/Kiss, or at a +6 true count w/Mentor)

2) **Using Kiss, change tables, hit the bathroom or take a break when you're 1½ decks into a six deck shoe if your running count is "4" or lower. With Mentor, leave <u>anytime</u> you reach a true count of -7 or lower.**

3) **Dedicate a partial segment of each play day to just plain "Wonging" in.**

PLAYING 2 HANDS

Many casual blackjack players routinely play two simultaneous hands. This of course all goes for naught, since it'll bring exactly the same results as two individual persons playing one hand apiece while using identical strategies. Think about it. If seat "A" plays perfect basic strategy, he has about a ½% disadvantage in a multi-deck game. If seat "B" plays the same way, he also has a ½% disadvantage. If both seats just happen to be the same person, *what difference can that possibly make?*

There are however, select occasions when a *card counter* can draw an advantage from playing two simultaneous hands! That's when the count is high -- providing there's at least one other player at the table. As an example, let's say you're in a three-handed game and your count suggests a five unit bet. About 11 cards will be used up on each round. Of those 11 cards, you will get *one* hand. If you go to two hands, about 14 cards will be used for each *two* hands you're dealt. If there's say, one deck left before the cut card comes out, you'll get in *5 hands* playing them *one at a time* and *8 hands* by playing *two at a time! By playing two spots, you'll get down more hands in this advantageous situation!*

This however, is not quite as good as it sounds since both of your hands are played against the same dealer's hand. That makes you somewhat more likely to win both, or lose both than if they were two completely separate hand scenarios -- which in turn increases your volatility. For this reason, when playing two hands you should *cut down* the amount wagered on each to about *70%* of what you'd play a single hand for. If your ten unit bet would be $100 for one hand, then two hands at $70 each would be an appropriate amount. That will adjust for the increased volatility of risking two bets against one dealer's hand, but;

YOU'LL STILL GET MORE TOTAL DOLLARS IN ACTION AS THE FAVORITE WHILE RUNNING THROUGH THAT SAME SUPPLY OF CARDS

That's because 8 hands at $70 each is $560 in action, but 5 hands at $100 each is only $500. The more players there are at the table, the more there is to be gained by going to two hands with positive counts! And if you go to *three* hands, then *$60* each rather than one *$100* wager is a good number.

If you're playing heads up though, *stay with just one hand through your strong counts!* Multiple hands here will use up more cards per dollar bet -- and you don't want to do that. Finally, remember this. On a "plus" count, if it appears the last round is coming up, you should go to 2 or even 3 hands *regardless* of the number of players! That's because you'll now be sucking an extra hand or two out of the pack that you never would have gotten.

180

THE RIGHT TIME TO QUIT

It's an age-old question. When have you made enough money to lock up your winnings for the day, and when is it time to cut your losses and throw in the towel? This extremely prevalent question is generally looked at so illogically by people who are otherwise sensible and logical, yet it has such a simple answer. That's because determining if it's time to quit has nothing to do with whether you're winning or losing! An excellent example can be taken from the highly skillful game of poker.

Suppose you sat down at a casino poker table with a crew of total strangers. After half an hour you realized you were playing with a table full of world class professionals. You were by far the weakest player, but you had made a couple of key hands and were winning. What should you do?

Since you'll almost certainly be beaten senseless if you continue to buck heads with them, you should definitely quit right now! And what if you were already losing? Same answer! Get out of there ASAP before they bleed you dry!

Now let's reverse it and say you've discovered you're playing with a bunch of complete suckers. You're head and shoulders above them all, but you've taken a few tough beats and are getting slaughtered! What should you do now?

Since you outclass the field, the "cream will eventually rise to the top" if you stick with it, so you should stay even though you're losing. And what if you were already winning? You're highly likely to keep right on winning, so again stay put!

Can you see that whether you should quit or keep gambling has nothing to do with how much you're winning or losing? Here are the sole determinants:

A) If you have the edge, you should always keep playing.
B) If you're the underdog, you should never have started,
   so quit right now!

Since it's impossible to accurately guess how fickle Lady Luck will behave over the upcoming short term, your best estimate is always based upon *your odds to win from this point going forward.* If you're "stuck like a pig" and feel as though getting even is hopeless, then forget about getting even! Your only

181

question should be, *"If I keep playing, am I likely to win money starting right now?"* If you're still playing well and game conditions remain okay, your chance to win a few bucks *starting now* are just as good as they'll be next week! But if you've been mentally upset by bad beats and can't shake it off, you'd best pack it in before you do something to beat *yourself.* Just realize that you'll have lost your edge by your own doing, and -- *that's a fault you need to work on!*

As for guessing the future, there is no *curve* that'll show you when your winning streak is ending. There's no *support level* at the bottom that'll predict a blackjack free-fall. *That stuff is all in your head!* Whether you keep playing, or quit and come back in a month, to the cards and chips, *it'll just be your next hand.* All your sessions will piggyback end-to-end, as if they were one long session anyway.

BANKROLLING

Simply playing blackjack with an advantage doesn't mean you can't hit a nasty losing streak and go broke. The best you can ever really do, is have enough bankroll to make that very unlikely.

That's where mathematical *risk of ruin* formulas come in handy. They can compute how many *units* it takes to have a high probability of surviving a sustained run of bad cards. So with the added help of John Auston's *BlackJack Risk Manager* software, here are 3 basic charts to tell you how much bankroll you should have;

for the **DAY**, for the **VACATION TRIP**, and for the **YEAR**

For the Day: Say you're headed to the casino for a 4-hour session. The following chart tells you roughly how many of your *maximum bets* to bring along, to give you various margins of safety. It's assumed you use *KISS II* or better, with a 1-to-6 betting spread in two-deck play, and 1-to-10 for the shoe, averaging 85 hands/hour.

BANKROLL NEEDED FOR 4 HOURS OF PLAY

	90% Safe	95% Safe	98% Safe
DOUBLE DECK	14 Max Bets	17 Max Bets	21 Max Bets
SHOE GAME	11 Max Bets	14 Max Bets	17 Max Bets

The bottom entry, middle row says you need 14 ten-unit bets to play the shoes for 4 hours and survive 19 days out of 20. Charts were computed for game conditions described on pages 193 and 194. For a more thorough coverage of applied "risk of ruin" bankrolling, see Don Schlesinger's *Blackjack Attack*.

Vacation Stake: What if you're going on a 4 or 5 day trip to blackjack country, and think you'll play 25 hours while there? How much loot do you need to play the same stakes over that period?

BANKROLL NEEDED FOR 25 HOURS OF PLAY

	90% Safe	95% Safe	98% Safe
DOUBLE DECK	34 Max Bets	41 Max Bets	50 Max Bets
SHOE GAME	28 Max Bets	33 Max Bets	40 Max Bets

Looking over the first two charts, notice that it takes only about $2^1/2$ times as much money to play 6 times as many hours. Actually, there's a simple "rule of thumb" you can use to quickly determine your bankroll for various sessions and vacation trips. It's called:

*The Square Root Rule: Once you know how much pocket money you need to play a single session, you can use square root to determine how much it takes to play several sessions. That's because your **standard deviation**, or **volatility**, runs proportional to the **square root** of the length of your play.*

For example, let's say you've learned that you need $1000 to comfortably play a 4 hour session. Then how much do you need to play the same stakes for 36 hours when you fly to Vegas next month? That would take about $3000. Why? Because the square root of 36 hours (which is 6) is triple the square root of 4 hours (which is 2).

With those two amounts of money, you'll have about the same chance of going broke in each scenario. For much longer periods though, such as 100 hours or more, the "square root rule" begins to break down. But for any two lengths of play between 3 hours and 50 hours, the rule is accurate enough for practical use, and comes in handy.

For the Year: Suppose you expect to play about 300 hours of blackjack this year. Then here's how much money you *could* end up needing if things should go bad for months on end.

BANKROLL NEEDED FOR 300 HOURS OF PLAY

	90% Safe	95% Safe	98% Safe
DOUBLE DECK	87 Max Bets	108 Max Bets	135 Max Bets
SHOE GAME	75 Max Bets	93 Max Bets	115 Max Bets

This chart assumes you cannot reload your bankroll if you do indeed "tap out" during the year. If you could, you wouldn't need as much money on hand in January. But even with a fixed bankroll, a player can virtually always choose to reduce his betting stakes once his reserve falls to a certain level. Thus, an advantage player should seldom if ever, be put entirely "out of business".

183

WILL COUNTING ERRORS ERASE YOUR EDGE?

Card counting can give you the overall advantage in blackjack by a slim margin of usually less than 1%. With such a razor thin edge, it seems natural to assume that you have to count, bet and play your hands flawlessly in order to win. So, what if you count cards and know your bets and index plays cold – but you miscount a few cards here and there? *Are you playing a losing game?*

Well, nobody plays *perfect* blackjack. So maybe it all boils down to how often you screw up, and by how much. To assess this worrisome concern, Stanford Wong's *Blackjack Count Analyzer* was rigged to run the *unbalanced KISS III* Count with six decks – but -- *be four cards off on the running count at all times!*

Rules were the same as game '*A*' on page 83. Bet spread was $25-to-$250 w/$50 off the top in a 3-handed game. The cutoff was $1^3/_4$ decks with wongouts at *perceived* running counts of '*4*' or less.

First, to establish a reference base the computer played 500 million hands properly, with the initial count correctly set at '*9*'.

Next, the initial count was deliberately set *four* points *low* at '*5*' rather than '*9*', and run for another 500 million hands. The bet ramp still began at a *perceived* '*20*' – now actually '*24*'. Insurance kicked in at '*29*' rather than a proper '*25*'. All other index plays and multi-unit bets tripped in four points late as well. Due to erring on the low side, the computer wonged out of about $^1/_4$ of the hands.

Finally, the initial count was *reset* to '*13*' rather than '*9*', thereby being constantly *four* points *high,* and run again. This induced many more multi-unit bets *(ramping up at an actual '16')* with some at negative EVs! Several premature index plays were also instigated while wongouts occurred only 3% of the time due to playing the moderately negative counts. All three results follow.

MODE OF PLAY	Avg. Result	Lose $3k in 3 hr.	Lose $25k in 300 hr.
Accurate Counting	Win $38 / hour	1 time in 15	4% chance
Always 4 points *Low*	Win $25 / hour	1 time in 160	½% chance
Always 4 points *High*	Win $42 / hour	1 time in 5	16% chance

Contrary to popular opinion, the sloppy counter didn't lose! His wins either shrank sharply or his bankroll risk shot skyward, *but he did retain some net advantage.* Can this make sense? We know the

183.1

essence of winning play is to bet lots more money at an advantage than when an underdog. So let's see how many *average* dollars per hour were bet at an advantage vs. when there was a disadvantage.

MODE OF PLAY	$ Bet w/ Advantage	$ Bet w/ Disadvantage	W / L
Accurate Counting	$3630	$1635	+$38
Always 4 points *Low*	$1920	$1305	+$25
Always 4 points *High*	$5995	$2360	+$42
Flat $50 Basic Strategy	$1410	$3590	-$24

Even when clearly off on the count, many more chips were bet as a favorite than as a '*dog*'. Note the *positive/negative* bet distributions for *any* counting mode in stark contrast to flat basic strategy. The counter's net gain from these disparities gets further amplified by making his largest bets when the player advantage is highest.

So then, what about miscounting cards with a *balanced* count? Could there be a different effect? For that matter, what might other simulation software come up with? To find out, the *balanced Hi/Lo* Count was hooked up to Norm Wattenberger's acclaimed *Casino Verite CVCX*. First came the baseline 500 million hand run with a '*0*' starting count, followed by another 500 million initiating at *-4,* then 500 million more beginning at *+4*. Those results are below.

MODE OF PLAY	Avg. Result	Lose $3k in 3 hr.	Lose $25k in 300 hr.
Accurate Counting	Win $39 / hour	1 time in 15	4% chance
Always 4 points *Low*	Win $24 / hour	1 time in 165	½% chance
Always 4 points *High*	Win $44 / hour	1 time in 5	15% chance

That's two different classes of count systems simulated with two software versions, both yielding very similar results. Let's reflect.

From the top of the shoe to the shuffle 4¼ decks in, a 4-card miscount causes conversion errors of 0.7 TC to 2.3 TC. These errors are apparently small enough that an ample bet spread with routine wongouts still yields a net player gain, *albeit smaller and riskier*.

As for double deck play; the same 4-card error brings miscues running beyond 5 TC -- just too much to fade! In double deck sims, a 2-card slip-up was about as costly as a 4-card error with the shoe. **SUMMARY:** Sloppy counting is a double whammy. You'll win less money and go belly up more often. But just for the record, if you do every other thing right except you often blow the count by only a few cards – you're probably *not* playing a losing game.

183.2

CAMOUFLAGE

If you were a flat bettor, you'd probably never have to worry about being spotted as a card counter. Since all kinds of goofs play their hands all kinds of goofy ways, even your expert plays of doubling down with *10* against an *Ace* wouldn't draw much attention. *No* -- it's that uncharacteristically *big bet* in conjunction with the unusual play that causes both the pit and surveillance to do a double-take.

So how are you going to get the big bets out there when you need to -- *and* make the key plays in the right spots? If you're a $10-to-$100 bettor in a shoe game, you usually won't have to worry about it. But if you're spreading $25-to-$250 or bigger, it'll eventually boil down to a matter of trade-offs. Now and then, you'll have to make a slightly bad play for a small wager in order to preserve the green light on a key custom play for the serious money. The trick is to;

MAKE BAD PLAYS THAT LOOK *TERRIBLE*, BUT ARE REALLY ONLY *SLIGHTLY BAD*

Lots of floor people might be sharp enough to spot a smart basic strategy departure when they see one. But very few can tell the difference between a horrible mistake and an insignificant one. Here's an example.

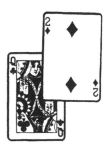

You've probably been around the game long enough to see somebody double down with that hand, haven't you? *What the heck"*, he says. *"I gotta hit it anyway -- I might as well double in case I catch a card".*

It's true, he's not changing the outcome of the hand, since he'll never want a second hit anyway. But he's doubling his bet as a 5-to-3 underdog! After all the wins, losses and ties blend together, he'll end up losing 25% of all the money he ever had riding on *12* against a *deuce*. For deciding that it seems like a good idea to double down, he's rightfully earned himself the reputation of a frigging *moron!*

How'd you like to have his image? To some degree, you probably can. How? Suppose the floorman happens to be looking your way when you've got *12* against a *deuce*. You've got a basic sized bet up there and would like for him to see you double down with that hand. So you do it -- *for less ---------- much less!* I mean;

IF YOU'VE GOT $25 RIDING ON *12* AGAINST A *DEUCE*, GO AHEAD AND DOUBLE FOR AN EXTRA BUCK!

How much is that going to cost you? We already said that on average, you'll lose 25% of everything you ever had riding on that hand. You can already color that money *gone.* So doubling for an extra dollar costs you another statistical *25 cents!* That's it! Even if the pit boss isn't there, the dealer will most likely call out, *"Doubling on a hard 12",* -- and you will have paid the bare bones minimum to look stupid. But your play wasn't nearly as stupid as doubling for the full amount!

There are lots of other dumb looking plays you can make which are small enough errors that their cost will be very little. Fifteen of them are listed on the next page. They're called *"the Nifty 15".*

You should *not* make these mistakes all the time. But even if you *did* make them on *all* your one unit bets *(when your average size bet was two units),* they would take roughly .04% off your overall net edge. Instead, just make them where they'll do the most good. *(The figures in the chart are for the shoe game and will vary modestly in one and two deck play).*

185

THE *NIFTY* 15

HAND	CAMOUFLAGE PLAY	COST TO A $25 BET	LOSS IN EDGE**
8 against a 6	Double	$0.50	-.002%
9 against a deuce	Double	$0.25	-.001%
11 against an Ace	Double	$0.55	-.003%
12 against a deuce	Double for $1	$0.25	-.003%
12 against a 3	Double for $1	$0.25	-.003%
12 against a 4	Double for $1	$0.20	-.002%
15 against a 10	Double for $1	$0.50	-.019%
A/7 against an Ace	Stand	$0.15	< -.001%
A/6 against a deuce	Double for $10	$0.10	< -.001%
A/7 against a deuce	Double (full)	$0.05	< -.001%
2/2 against an 8	Split	$0.40	< -.001%
3/3 against an 8	Split	$0.25	< -.001%
7/7 against an 8	Split	$0.25	< -.001%
9/9 against an Ace	Split	$0.75	< -.001%
Insure a 20	$5 worth	$0.45	-.006%
			-.04%

Roughly one out of every sixteen hands you're dealt will be one of those listed above. Some come up often, others once in a great while. All three soft hands along with the four pairs appear so seldom that their combined loss is only around .002%. But remember, **the chart considers that you make these camouflage plays whenever they come up on your one unit bets only!* If you used "camo" at every opportunity regardless of bet size, the total cost would be a roughly double.

The last play on the list, insuring a *20* for less is worth talking about. I prefer it to taking "even money" on blackjack. Insuring a *20* for 1/5 of the bet is less than half as costly as even money, looks dumber and presents itself more than twice as often.

Also, suppose you're playing two hands at $25 apiece, but the count isn't high enough for Insurance and the dealer has an *Ace* up. In this spot you might occasionally want to insure the better of the two hands for five or ten bucks. If your true count is "+2", your disadvantage *(and cost)* is only a third of what it normally would be. It looks good and is pretty cheap cover.

TABLE IMAGE

Once you find a not too crowded blackjack table with playable rules and decent penetration, you need to be able to sit down and play without being subjected to anti-card-counting measures. The casinos know that fundamentally, blackjack can be beaten. They also know that not one gambler in a hundred, perhaps a thousand can play well enough to get the job done. But if they think you might be that one player, *you will draw heat!*

The floor people will begin to observe your play very closely. The cut card will probably be placed further from the bottom of the shoe, or deck. Some pit persons may actually count right along with you and have the dealer shuffle up when the deck goes positive, even if the cut card hasn't come out yet! They can tape you from the surveillance room and re-evaluate your play later. You might have your picture taken from several angles and never be aware of it. The pit boss may drastically reduce the maximum betting limit at your table. And when you move to another table, the limit may be reduced there too, and brought back to normal at the table you just vacated. In the state of Nevada, they can flat out tell you to leave!

These are all things you must learn to avoid in order to not give up your edge. Playing unimpeded often requires a convincing "dumb act". You need to blend in with the average sucker. You want to act how *he* acts. You want to say what *he* would say in your position. That's what is meant by *"table image"*. When you play, try not to appear very serious about what you're doing. Following is a list of personality traits that you should try to exude at the table. These, combined with an occasional camouflage play will go a long way towards covering up the real you.

◆ It'll help if you make a joke of it when you lose a big bet. *And you will lose some big bets!* So when you hit *16* against an *8* and bust with a *10*, you might occasionally show a little sportsmanship by jesting something like, *"Twenty-six so far; okay, hit me again!"*

◆ It can be good for your image if you appear to be drinking. Ice water in a cocktail glass with a squeeze of lime isn't a bad idea.

Always try to appear loose and relaxed, as though you came to "gamble it up".

◆ Sometimes, it's not a bad idea to ask for advice from the dealer or other players at the table on how they would play one of your close hands -- then thank them if you win.

◆ When making an unusual, but strategically astute play, you may need to express some shallow reason for doing it as a decoy. For example, when doubling down with *Ace/8* against a *6,* you might clarify that you always soft double against a "bust" card, ignoring the fact that you already have *19.*

◆ If the count goes positive at a multi-handed table and you want to "hog" more of those cards for yourself by playing two hands, you might say something like, *"Man, she's killin' us! Lemme' put in another hand and change the cards around".*

◆ When you move to a new table and plop down your chips, often times the dealer or another player will ask, *"How's it going today?"* Sometimes you could answer, *"Having one of my best days ever; only stuck $500!"*

◆ When you're not at third base and the other players have stayed pat with stiffs, if the dealer breaks you could mutter some nonsense about the third baseman having "saved the table". It can also be good for your image if you "high-five" the player next to you every once in a while after the dealer breaks.

◆ If you play repeatedly at the same casino, it doesn't look good if your stack of chips often seems to be growing. You need to smoothly remove some of them from the table *every time* you play. *Do not* however, remove the any of the largest denomination chip for that table. Those are usually tracked pretty closely.

One cautionary word about table image. Don't overdo it. Sometimes you can get carried away with your little act and bring attention to yourself that you never would have gotten playing it straight. If you manage your hands like you know exactly what you're doing, and act like a complete idiot at the same time you may look more suspicious than anybody. But still, these are all things you should be able to do when the situation calls for it.

MAINTAINING POISE

Be forewarned. Even if you have the $3/4$% edge of a true blackjack expert, you're *still gambling!* Some days you'll labor through your whole act; phony drinks, silly jokes and all just to keep your welcome mat in place. And what'll happen? *You'll get your doors blown off as if you really are the sucker you were pretending to be!* It'll make you wonder what you were trying to protect in the first place. When things go wrong like this, maintaining your winning *poise* is critical!

Don't start brooding; *"I just can't win a hand; I double with a monster count to make 20 against a 5, and she pulls a six card 21 to blister me for another two hundred bucks! Un-effing-believable!"*

Well, it's not unbelievable! It's all part of the game! When such events persist you'll be tempted to change gears and try something you know is not proper. Well, don't even think about it, because;

**IF YOU BREAK PROPER FORM IN AN EFFORT
TO CHANGE THE RESULTS, YOU'RE MORE
LIKELY TO CHANGE THEM FOR THE WORSE!**

It's all one long gambling game landscaped with hills and valleys. You're on a continuous journey that'll consume countless days and nights. Some nights you'll park and rest on a hill, other nights in a valley. But either way, you're on the right road. *Stay on it!*

Shoe games can be particularly testy. You might hang close to even for hours while patiently counting through neutral and negative shoes, then get whacked for 30 units on the next few "high-count" hands! And what's your move when the shuffle comes? *Go back into your shell, revert to the small bets and wait obediently for the next positive shoe!* If it doesn't come, it doesn't come! Don't break form no matter what! *Gambling is very tough on undisciplined gamblers.*

If you're supremely disciplined, can tolerate some nasty beatings along the way, and can play your game accurately and convincingly, then you'll *most likely* net some extra spending cash from playing blackjack. As for living the life of luxury constantly knocking down the big bucks? Not likely! As I said before:

IT CAN BE ONE TOUGH WAY TO MAKE SOME EASY MONEY!

Chapter 11
KEY POINTS

1) Gaining the upper hand at blackjack is a two step process; learning to beat the **game** and learning to beat the **house.**

2) All blackjack games are not "beatable". The rules, decks and dealing procedures are all contributing factors that can make a game "good" or "bad".

3) Of the three variables listed above, the most subtle is "dealing procedure".

4) "Deck penetration" can be worth more than 1/2% in overall expectation to a card counter.

5) Crowded tables not only slow down your play, but also contribute to shallower overall effective penetration.

6) The betting spread a card counter needs in order to maintain an advantage escalates dramatically as the number of decks increases.

7) A card counter must learn to skew more high cards in his direction by leaving tables with poor counts.

8) Playing on an inadequate bankroll is a near sure way to stop a winning system from working.

9) The card counter must establish a typical gambler's "table image" so as to avoid anti-card-counting countermeasures from the casino. This involves exuding a recreational personality, as well as occasionally making an incorrect play.

10) Without supreme discipline, fortitude and character, a card counter cannot succeed even though he may possess every other scientific and artful skill.

12

*the*Mentor Count*

All the counting systems described thus far in this book have been of the "unbalanced" structure. They've also been "level one" counts in that each counted card is either plus or minus one point. You can get moderately better performance than what those systems offer, but the complexity will go up faster than the performance. The system described in this chapter is a top notch "level two" balanced count. If you're not rather obsessed with the game of casino "21", it's most likely not for you. But if you're truly exhilarated by the mental gymnastics of juggling numbers in your head to tell you how to bet your money and play your hands more efficiently, then by all means read on.

Nearly every card that is played out of the deck or shoe has an effect on your chances to win the following hand. The cards that help the dealer when they are still in the pack are the *2, 3, 4, 5, 6,* and *7*. The cards that help the player are the *9, 10, Jack, Queen, King* and *Ace*. The *8* is virtually meaningless. So in all, there are six dealer-helping cards and six player-helping cards.

In an effort to make your card count more thorough, you could try counting all the *2's* through *7's* as +1, and the *9's* through

Aces as -1. But that's far from optimal since some cards make a lot more difference than others when they're played out.

That's where the *multi-level* card count concept entered the picture. In the 1960's, Edward O. Thorp of *"Beat the Dealer"* fame developed his *"Ultimate Point Count"* for detecting with total accuracy where the betting advantage lies as cards are dealt out of play. Each card was counted with a plus or minus value in direct proportion to its own significance. For example, the most important card in the deck, the *five* was counted as +11. *Deuces* were +5 and all the *tens* were -7. The other cards had their own assigned values as well. So, on the multi-level card count scale the Ultimate Point Count was regarded as a *"level eleven"* count system. It was 100% efficient -- but practically 100% unusable.

Still, Thorp had a heck of a concept going. Since then, several other less radical multi-level card counting systems have been devised in an attempt to accurately monitor the ever-shifting percentages in blackjack. Two, three and four level systems were designed and marketed in the 1970's and '80's with claims of being devastatingly powerful in casino play.

However, hindsight once again proved to be the best judge. Subsequent computer programs were developed to test the performance of card counting systems, both simple and complex. They revealed that due to the natural law of diminishing returns it hardly pays to get super-sophisticated. A well-designed *single* level card count turned out to yield about 90% as much mathematical advantage as a well-designed level *four* system.

COMPARATIVE PERFORMANCES of BLACKJACK COUNT SYSTEMS

To learn just how much better some count systems can be than others, I ran billions of computer simulated blackjack hands with more than two dozen card counts. The results revealed that;

IF YOU'RE REALLY SERIOUS ABOUT BLACKJACK AND WANT YOUR CARD COUNT TO YIELD THE MAXIMUM PRACTICAL EDGE, USE A GOOD LEVEL TWO SYSTEM.

Level one systems are fine. Level two systems can produce up to a 10% higher edge. With level three systems you might get another 3%, and beyond that -- forget it! The table below lists 16 of the counting systems that were tested.

count system	2	3	4	5	6	7	8	9	10	J	Q	K	A	Bet	Play
KISS Count*	0/1	0	1	1	1	0	0	0	0	-1	-1	-1	0	79%	51%
Stage II Kiss Ct*	0/1	1	1	1	1	0	0	0	-1	-1	-1	-1	0	89%	61%
Stage III Kiss Ct*	0/1	1	1	1	1	1	0	0	-1	-1	-1	-1	-1	96%	55%
Red 7 Count*	1	1	1	1	1	1/0	0	0	-1	-1	-1	-1	-1	97%	53%
Black Ace Count*	1	1	1	1	1	0	0	0	-1	-1	-1	-1	-1/0	93%	55%
KO Count*	1	1	1	1	1	1	0	0	-1	-1	-1	-1	-1	97%	55%
Hi/Lo Count	1	1	1	1	1	0	0	0	-1	-1	-1	-1	-1	97%	51%
Silver Fox System	1	1	1	1	1	1	0	-1	-1	-1	-1	-1	-1	96%	54%
Hi Opt II Count	1	1	2	2	1	1	0	0	-2	-2	-2	-2	0	91%	67%
Omega II Count	1	1	2	2	2	1	0	-1	-2	-2	-2	-2	0	92%	67%
Zen Count	1	1	2	2	2	1	0	0	-2	-2	-2	-2	-1	96%	63%
Revere Point Ct	1	2	2	2	2	1	0	0	-2	-2	-2	-2	-2	98%	55%
Mentor Count	1	2	2	2	2	1	0	-1	-2	-2	-2	-2	-1	97%	62%
Unbalanced Zen*	1	2	2	2	2	1	0	0	-2	-2	-2	-2	-1	96%	62%
Wong Halves	1	2	2	3	2	1	0	-1	-2	-2	-2	-2	-2	99%	56%
Uston SS Count*	2	2	2	3	2	1	0	-1	-2	-2	-2	-2	-2	99%	55%

The software used for running the following count system analysis, *(as well as most of the other computer work in this book)* was *Stanford Wong's Blackjack Count Analyzer*. It recorded each count's overall performance, it's dollar earnings and the standard deviation *(luck factor)*. Each system was run for a total of 500 million hands. First, 300 million hands were played with six decks, then another 200 million with two decks. The rules for the six deck runs were as follows:

DEALER STANDS ON SOFT 17
DOUBLE ON ANY STARTING HAND
DOUBLE AFTER SPLIT
NO RE-SPLITTING OF ANY PAIRS
NO SURRENDER

The basic strategy house edge was 0.48%. All hands were played "heads up". The cut card placement was at $1^3/4$ decks in the shoe

193

games with a 1-to-10 betting spread.   In double deck play the dealer *hit* soft *17*, but *re-splitting* of normal pairs *was allowed* for a basic strategy house edge of 0.42%. The last 42 cards were cut off and a "2-1-6" spread was used.

Count systems with an asterisk after their names are unbalanced counts. The far right hand columns in the table on page 193 give each system's betting correlation and hand playing efficiency. The results for all 16 count systems are printed below.

Count System	2 Deck Yield	6 Deck Yield
KISS Count*	+.45%	+.48%
Stage II Kiss Ct*	+.63%	+.64%
Stage III Kiss Ct*	+.69%	+.70%
Red 7 Count*	+.68%	+.71%
Black Ace Count*	+.66%	+.67%
KO Count*	+.69%	+.68%
Hi/Lo Count	+.74%	+.72%
Silver Fox System	+.72%	+.71%
Hi Opt II Count	+.80%	+.72%
Omega II Count	+.79%	+.74%
Zen Count	+.81%	+.77%
Revere Point Ct	+.79%	+.76%
Mentor Count	+.82%	+.77%
Unbalanced Zen*	+.73%	+.72%
Wong Halves	+.81%	+.78%
Uston SS Count*	+.75%	+.74%

Statistically, there's a 95% chance that each result is within 0.02% of that system's true ability. The main criterion for this comparison was to keep the standard deviation at the same level for all systems, so that in play everybody encountered equal volatility. As a by-product, all count systems had virtually the same size average bet. *The fact that the higher performing systems could bet a little more money with the same overall risk of ruin was ignored for this test -- since that would not change their EV percentages.*

As you can see, there is not a great deal of difference between the performance of a good simple count and a good complex one. But there is *some* difference! Furthermore, notice that most of the increase in performance comes when you upgrade from level one to level two. Notice also, that some of the count systems keep track of the *Ace* while others ignore it. Why?

Card counting systems have two separate facets to their usefulness. The first is to determine when the player has an advantage on the next hand due to the high/low strength of the cards that remain. This is called the system's *betting correlation*. The second facet indicates when it's better to play your hand contrary to the basic strategy, again because of the remaining cards. This is known as the count's *playing efficiency*. These two aspects of card counting are dealt with in greater detail in Peter Griffin's book, *"The Theory of Blackjack"*.

Unfortunately, the two characteristics sometimes work against each other. That's because the *Ace* is actually a "high/low" card. Sometimes it counts as *1* in the hand and sometimes as *11*. For that reason, counting the *Ace* along with the high cards is liable to mislead you in the play of your hand. A classic example would be when you're doubling down. If you have *9* or *10*, catching a high card, particularly an *Ace* would be awesome. But if you're doubling down with *11*, buying an *Ace* is *the kiss of death!* Hence, some system designers believe the *Ace* should be ignored by the main count altogether, and kept track of separately for betting purposes alone.

Still, others insist that since the *Ace* is crucial in determining when the player has the edge in the game, it mustn't be ignored but indeed counted as a precious high card, first and foremost.

Both arguments have merit. But overall, a card count's *betting* accuracy is more important than its *playing* accuracy. That's largely because strategic opportunities to increase your bet arise much more often than those occasions when you should "change-up" the play of your hand. The more decks you're playing with, the more this is so.

Then what's the answer? The "hot setup" would be to just keep a separate count of *Aces* and adjust your main count for betting purposes when those *Aces* got out of kilter. Admittedly, that would be a lot of extra work considering the extra potential gain. This is what led me to begin fabricating new multi-level balanced

195

counts on the computer, first including then ignoring the *Ace*. Using Griffin's equations as design parameters, my goal was to derive a "one-size-fits-all" count system that would perform admirably in both shoe and hand held games -- *without the use of any side counts*. After roughly a billion hands of hit and miss, I finally struck on a level two structure which eclipsed the performance of all other level two systems, and was on a par with level three counts as a whole. This, I affectionately dubbed, *the Mentor Count*.

The *Mentor Count* is a complete "level two" balanced system with tables of index numbers that tell you when to vary your play from the basic strategy with roughly 80 different hands. As the chart on page 194 shows, it outperforms the vast majority of fully structured count systems on the public market today, *regardless of complexity*. This count probably represents the practical upper limit for card counting systems *that do not employ a separate side-count of other cards*. The accuracy ratings of the *Mentor Count* are as follows:

Betting Correlation	**97%**
Playing Efficiency	**62%**

This superb mix makes the *Mentor Count* an excellent *"all-around-athlete"* for playing blackjack effectively against any number of decks without the added use of any side-counts. A graphic of the *Mentor Count* is illustrated below:

The Mentor Count

CARD RANK

2	3	4	5	6	7	8	9	10	A
+1	+2	+2	+2	+2	+1	0	-1	-2	-1

Notice that the *Mentor Count* does include all the *Aces*, but counts them with less impact than each of the *10's*. This was a key factor in achieving its high all-around performance. Integrating the *deuce*, 7 and 9 with less value than the other more vital cards is also appropriate. Thus, the *Mentor Count* tracks virtually every card in the deck that matters *(the 8 does have minuscule value for playing the hand, but is nil for betting purposes)*.

You may also notice that the *Mentor Count* is structured and performs very similarly to the excellent *Zen Count*. In the real world, there will never be any perceptible difference in net gain from using one over the other. With the *Mentor* however, there are 20 two card combinations that cancel each other out, such as;

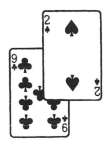  

where with the *Zen*, there are just 16. If like most card counters, you count cards two at a time, the *Mentor Count* may run a tad smoother at the tables.

BALANCED COUNTING

Unlike the *Kiss Counts*, the *Mentor* system is a *balanced* card count. That is, all the small cards add up to +10 while the big cards total -10. This equality is necessary in order to more accurately determine your betting advantage or disadvantage at *all* counts and when to take Insurance. A balanced count is also needed for indicating when to make many "off-the-wall" plays like standing with *15* against a *9* or hitting *14* against a *deuce*.

When using any balanced system, you do not "pre-load" your initial count at the beginning of play with some positive number *(such as starting a six deck shoe with a count of "9")*. Instead, the nearly universal method is to begin at "even", or "zero" regardless of how many decks are used. As the small cards come out, you add 1 or 2 points to your count depending upon the card. With each big card that appears, subtract 1 or 2 points for each.

197

With the *Mentor Count* for example -- starting at "zero", if the first card off the top of the pack was a *9*, your running count would move to -1. If the next six cards were;

your count would have gone from -1 to;

+1,   -1,   0,   +1,   -1,   -2

One of the trickiest things to do with a balanced count is to not mess up the running total when crossing back and forth from a positive to a negative count. As if that's not problematic enough, now the cocktail waitress may stop by and ask if you need a drink. It wouldn't take much at all to inadvertently pick up the count at +2 instead of -2 at the start of the next hand.

A "100" COUNTING BASE

Because of that, I always begin my count off the top of a new pack at "100". When that *9* was the first card out, my running count would go to "99", *(meaning negative 1)*. Now, when those same next six cards were played, my count would run:

101, 99, 100, 101, 99, 98

I simply count forward and backward from 100. I never have to fool with "minuses" and there's no risk of accidentally changing signs between hands. This has been my method for twenty-five years. I find it to be smoother and less error-prone. Just be aware that *a count of "92" really means "-8"!* In multi-deck play, the running count will sometimes get very far from "even". When this happens, you need to be comfortable with the idea that a count of

198

"**68**" is actually "**-32**". But don't worry, even with eight decks you will hardly ever reach the ambiguous count of "**50**" in either direction.

After a short while, you'll feel comfortable dropping the *"hundred"* off a *"one-o-four"* count, and simply count "4, 3, 2, 1, 0, 99, 98, etc.". If you don't think this is easier, then stick to the conventional method of starting at "zero" and going into minus running counts. But either way, you must be able to count down a full single deck in 30 seconds maximum, or you're not ready.

the TRUE COUNT

The most confusing aspect of balanced card counting is converting to the *"true count"*. Just what is the true count?

At the beginning of play with any number of full decks there are as many low cards *(2 through 7)* as high cards *(9 through Ace)*. When you get let's say, two decks into a six deck shoe, what would it mean if you had a running count of +**10** *(or "110")*? Think about it. With the *Mentor Count, (since the six low ranks of cards add up to ten points)* it would mean that about six more *low* cards have come out than **high** cards. This in turn means there are six more **high** cards left in the shoe than *low* cards. With four decks of cards still remaining, that would put the theoretical *total* of available cards at;

99 high cards
16 eights
93 low cards

But what if you still had a running count of +**10** after the dealer was nice enough to deal five full decks out? Now with only one deck left, the remaining supply of cards should be;

27 high cards
4 eights
21 low cards

In both cases there's a six card surplus of high ones. But in the first example, the *ratio* of available high-to-low cards is only 51%/49% -- and in the second case it's 56%/44%! Considering that

199

this ratio will hover around 50/50 during play, the second case is much more extreme! Yet in both cases the running count is "+10".

BY ADJUSTING THE RUNNING COUNT IN PROPORTION TO HOW MANY DECKS REMAIN, YOU GET WHAT'S KNOWN AS THE "TRUE COUNT"

The "true count" simply gives you an accurate indication of the *proportional* high/low strength of the remaining cards. That's the information you're really looking for.

Just how do you make this adjustment? There are several ways. Most methods involve *division*, but I prefer to *multiply*. I always *calibrate,* or "true up" my running count to *two decks.* That is, I want to bet my chips and play my hands according to how many high cards there are *per every two decks* that are left. There are a couple of reasons why I prefer this method.

First, the vast majority of blackjack games are six and eight deck shoes. Both generally get shuffled somewhere near the two remaining deck mark. Now the most critical point in any game is near the shuffle. If you're "truing up" to two decks;

THE TRUE COUNT AND THE RUNNING COUNT WILL BE CLOSE TO THE SAME AS THINGS COME DOWN TO "CRUNCH TIME",

thereby minimizing your conversion work dramatically. Second, many index numbers don't really fall right on a whole number, but somewhere in between. These are either rounded off, or truncated downward. By truing up to two decks, all your index numbers get doubled, *making them more accurate.*

It works the same way with sizing your bets. Using the old "count per deck" truing method, you might want to bet 3 units at "+1½" true. But truing up to two decks makes +1½ equal to +3! Furthermore, since the average card counts for 1⅔ points with the *Mentor Count,* all the values get increased even further, making +1½ high cards per deck equal to **+5** true *(true being "per two decks")!* It all gives you finer increments to work with -- *and they're all at whole numbers.*

So how are you going to make this critical adjustment on the fly? To do that straightaway, you'd have to divide the running count by the number of "double decks" that remain. That would be a snap if there were two decks left, and a *pain in the butt* if there were 3 1/2 decks left.

Going through these mental gyrations at the table is not something you want to mess with if you don't have to – and you *don't!* All you really have to do is become familiar with the chart shown below. It contains multipliers for converting the running count to the true count with just about any number of decks remaining.

TRUE COUNT CONVERSION CHART

REMAINING DECKS	MULTIPLIER
$^1/_2$	4
$^2/_3$	3
$^3/_4$	$2^1/_2$
1	2
$1^1/_4$	1.6
$1^1/_2$	$1^1/_3$
2	**1**
$2^1/_2$	.8
3	$^2/_3$
$3^1/_2$	.6
4	.5
5	.4
6	$^1/_3$
7	.3
8	$^1/_4$

It makes no difference how many decks you started with. Just begin each new shoe using the multiplier for the total number of decks in your game -- then move *up* the ladder as the discard tray fills *(i.e. for a 6 deck game, begin with a $^1/_3$ multiplier)*. Doing that,

THE RUNNING COUNT x THE MULTIPLIER FOR THOSE REMAINING DECKS WILL GIVE YOU THE TRUE COUNT

which is a literal indicator of the *high-to-low ratio* of the pack you're currently playing from. Now let's take it through a few examples together:

◆ Five decks left -- running count is +10:
  .4 x +10 = **+4** true count

◆ Three decks left -- running count is -18:
  $2/3$ of -18 = **-12** true count

◆ Two decks left -- running count is +13:
  with 2 decks left, the **R/C** always = the **T/C**

◆ Two-thirds of a deck left -- running count is +9:
  3 x +9 = **+27** true count

Remember, as cards are coming out you apply them to your *running count*. Then you must keep that running count in the back of your mind while you convert to the *true count* to size your bet or play your hand. After you've done that, pick up the running count again and update it as cards come into play.

How will you know how many decks are left? The discard tray is your source of information. By now you should be an astute judge of how many cards are in a given stack. Two decks of cards stand just about *nine* chips tall. During play, whatever is in the discard tray plus a bit more for the cards on the board will leave the remainder in the shoe. A little practice at home will teach you to gauge the remaining cards reasonably well.

Caution! Be careful about deviating from the basic strategy after you've converted to the true count! Realize that you're always *estimating* how many decks remain, plus your multiplication may be less than perfect. Because of this, it might be prudent to see the true count exceed the index number *(shown later)* for that particular hand by 10 or 15% before you "change up" your play. In that way you don't run the risk of playing worse than a basic strategy player. Sizing your bet is not as sensitive. Either you'll have an edge or you won't. It's not as big a deal if you mistakenly bet 4 units when you really should have only bet 3. You had the advantage either way. The most important part of sizing your bet according to the true count is making sure you indeed have an edge before you increase your bet. When you're not sure, a two unit wager might be a good idea. That will either be mathematically appropriate, or good for table image purposes.

BETTING and PLAYING STRATEGY
for the MENTOR COUNT

This is the heart of the *Mentor Count* system; betting your money and playing your hands. With any card count you generally want to start betting multiple units when the count has risen high enough to erase your handicap and give you an advantage of about $4/10\%$. In an average game, this generally occurs at a true count of **+5** or **+6** with the *Mentor* system. Each point in true count will change your advantage by about $1/8\%$. Use the "rules variations" table from Chapter 5 to adjust your betting schedule with uncommon rules/decks.

The betting schedule outlined below tells you how to bet your money with any number of decks. It's calibrated for average quality blackjack games with average rules and average penetration.

BETTING SCHEDULE for the MENTOR COUNT

TRUE COUNT	SINGLE DECK	DOUBLE DECK	4 DECKS	6 DECKS	8 DECKS
off the top	2u	2u	2u	1-2u	1-2u
thru +5	1u	1u	1u	1u	1u
+6	2u	2u	3u	3u	3u
+7	3u	3u	5u	5u	5u
+8	4u	4u	8u	8u	8u
+10	4u	6u	9u	10u	10u
+12	4u	6u	9u	10u	12u

Also remember that you should tend to walk away from a good number of shoes where the true count descends to around **-7** or worse.

VARIABLE STRATEGY
INDEX NUMBERS

With the *Kiss Counts* there were no more than twenty hands *(plus Insurance)* you would play differently from basic strategy between the running counts of "5" and "30". What you didn't concern yourself with, was the fact that there were also several other hands that could have been played more accurately at counts above and below that.

With the true count feature used in the *Mentor* system, you'll have an effective indicator of your advantage *(or handicap)* across a much broader range of counts. With the true count you'll be aware of some rare times that it'll actually be best to double down with *8* against a *4*, hit *14* against a *4* and even split a pair of *10's* against a *4!*

Following is your master strategy chart for the *Mentor Count*. Each index number within the boxes indicates the *true count* at which it becomes better to play that particular hand contrary to the basic strategy. If the box is merely shaded, then always play that hand according to the basic strategy.

HIT / STAND TABLE
IF THE TRUE COUNT IS EQUAL TO, OR MORE POSITIVE
THAN THE INDEX NUMBER, STAND: OTHERWISE HIT.
(Use Basic Strategy for all shaded squares)

DEALER'S UP-CARD

HAND	2	3	4	5	6	7	8	9	10	A
12	13	7	0	-7	-4*					
13	-2	-6	-11	-17	-17					
14	-12	-15	-20							
15								30	15	
16								22	1	30*
17										

*IF DEALER HITS SOFT 17, THEN: 12 vs. 6 is: -12, and 16 vs. ACE is: +15.

Look at the box that corresponds with *12* against a dealer's *2* up. The index number is **13**. The basic strategy says to hit *12* against

204

a *deuce*. But if the true count is **+13** or more positive, it would be better to stand with this hand. Now look at *14* against a *4*. Notice that its index number is **-20**. If the true count is more negative than **-20**, you should take a card rather than stand.

Throughout the "HIT/STAND" table, if the true count is more negative than the index number you should hit. If it is equal to or more positive than the number, you should stand. In any shaded squares, you will always follow the basic strategy.

Notice also, that some of the index numbers are very small, such as with *12* against a *4,* or *16* against a *10* up. These are hands that you'll be changing your play with regularly. When playing your hands by the true count, forget about more preliminary rules such as hand composition or board composition. The true count supersedes everything.

DOUBLE DOWN TABLE
IF THE TRUE COUNT IS EQUAL TO, OR MORE POSITIVE
THAN THE INDEX NUMBER, DOUBLE DOWN: OTHERWISE HIT.
(Use Basic Strategy for all shaded squares)

DEALER'S UP-CARD

HAND	2	3	4	5	6	7	8	9	10	A
8			21	13	7					
9	3	-3	-9	-16		12	30			
10								-17	-7	15	15
11								-18	-15	3*

*IF DEALER HITS SOFT 17, THEN, 11 vs. ACE is: -2

To use an example from the double down table, double with *9* against a *7* up if the true count is **+12** or more positive, otherwise follow the basic strategy and hit.

Also notice that there is occasionally an asterisk (*) in an index box. These are hands that are affected by the dealer's *"soft 17"* rule. The number inside the box assumes the dealer stands on *soft 17.* If the dealer hits a *soft 17,* the number that replaces it is given at the bottom of the table.

205

SOFT DOUBLING TABLE

IF THE TRUE COUNT IS EQUAL TO, OR MORE POSITIVE
THAN THE INDEX NUMBER, DOUBLE DOWN.
(Use Basic Strategy for all shaded squares)

DEALER'S UP-CARD

HAND	2	3	4	5	6	7	8	9	10	A
A/2			12	0	-8					
A/3			7	-10						
A/4			-2	-18						
A/5		10	-7							
A/6	4	-10	-20							
A/7	3	-6	-18							HIT / STD 3*
A/8		19	11	5	3*					
A/9			22	18	17					

*IF DEALER HITS SOFT 17, then A/8 vs. 6 is: -1 and ALWAYS HIT A/7 vs. A

Out at the lower right hand area of the soft doubling table, the "3*" in the box pertains to *hitting* and *standing* with *Ace/7* vs. an *Ace*, rather than doubling down. If the dealer stands on *soft 17*, hit unless the true count is +3 or greater, then stand. But if the dealer hits on *soft 17*, then *always* hit this hand.

PAIR SPLITTING

(WITHOUT "DOUBLE AFTER SPLIT")
IF THE TRUE COUNT IS EQUAL TO, OR MORE
POSITIVE THAN THE INDEX NUMBER, SPLIT.
(Use Basic Strategy for all shaded squares)

DEALER'S UP-CARD

HAND	2	3	4	5	6	7	8	9	10	A
2/2	25	9	-2	-14						
3/3		12	-3	-14						
4/4										
6/6	6	-5	-12	-20						
7/7										
8/8									(25)	
9/9	-4	-9	-13	-20	-20	30				24
10/10		30	22	18	17					
A/A										-20

(25) - USE IN REVERSE: IF TRUE COUNT EXCEEDS +25, DON'T SPLIT

One hand in the pair splitting table is acted upon in reverse. With a pair of *8's* against a *10* up, keep splitting *until* the true count rises to **+25**, then *stand*.

Also, as you might intuitively guess, when the true count is too negative to split, some pairs should be hit while others should be stood with. For that, follow the "hit/stand" table. A rare example is a pair of *6's* against a *4* up. If the true count were, let's say **-15**, you should no longer split; but you should also no longer stand since the index number for *12* against a *4* is "**0**"! Usually however, when a hand should no longer be split, the basic strategy applies.

PAIR SPLITTING
(WITH "DOUBLE AFTER SPLIT")
IF THE TRUE COUNT IS EQUAL TO, OR MORE
POSITIVE THAN THE INDEX NUMBER, SPLIT.
(Use Basic Strategy for all shaded squares)

DEALER'S UP-CARD

HAND	2	3	4	5	6	7	8	9	10	A
2/2	-12	-17								
3/3	-3									
4/4		30	12	-2	-7					
6/6	-6	-13	-20							
7/7							15			
8/8									(25)	
9/9	-10	-15	-19			18				18
10/10		30	22	18	17					
A/A										-20

(25) - USE IN REVERSE: IF TRUE COUNT EXCEEDS +25, DON'T SPLIT

When you can double down after splits, not only are there more pairs that should in fact be split, but the margin by which you should split many pairs becomes greater. That's because you might catch a card that will give you a good doubling hand, which makes splitting more advantageous than it was before. In some cases your pair will upgrade from a *defensive* split *(splitting reduces your overall loss)* to an *offensive* split *(splitting earns a net profit)* when you can double after splitting. Such a pair would be 2/2 against a dealer's 4.

207

SURRENDER
IF THE TRUE COUNT IS EQUAL TO OR MORE
POSITIVE THAN THE INDEX NUMBER, SURRENDER
(Use Basic Strategy for all shaded squares)

DEALER'S UP-CARD

HAND	8	9	10	A (STAND SOFT 17)	A (HIT SOFT 17)
13			27		
14		20	10	17	10
15	28	9	-1	6	-2
16	18	0	-10	-6	-20
17					(7)
8/8		30	6		*

(7) - USE IN REVERSE: SURRENDER UP TO +7,
THEN STAND.
*WITH 1 OR 2 DECKS ALWAYS SPLIT: WITH 4 TO
8 DECKS ALWAYS SURRENDER.

The surrender option is significantly affected by the *soft 17* rule. When the dealer has an *Ace* up, $1/13$th of the time she'll turn up a *6* from underneath giving her a *soft 17*. Consequently, there are two separate columns for when to surrender against an *Ace* showing.

INSURANCE: Take Insurance whenever the true count is +13 or more

On the following page is a condensed pocket size version of the *Mentor Variable Playing Strategy*. You can photocopy it, laminate it and carry it with you.

Double After Split IS allowed		DOUBLE		STAND			SPLIT		
	2	3	4	5	6	7	8	9	10	A

	2	3	4	5	6	7	8	9	10	A
8			21	13	7					
9	3	-3	-9	-16		12	30			
10							-17	-7	15	15
11								-18	-15	3*
12	13	7	0	-7	-4*					
13	-2	-6	-11	-17	-17					
14	-12	-15	-20							
15								30	15	
16								22	1	30*
A/2			12	0	-8					
A/3			7	-10						
A/4			-2	-18						
A/5		10	-7							
A/6	4	-10	-20							
A/7	3	-6	-18							3*
A/8		19	11	5	3*					
A/9			22	18	17					
2/2	-12	-17								
3/3	-3									
4/4		30	12	-2	-7					
6/6	-6	-13	-20							
7/7							15			
8/8									(25)	
9/9	-10	-15	-19			18				18
10's		30	22	18	17					
A/A										-20

surrender

14	20	10	17
15	9	-1	6
16	0	-10	-6

the VALUE of a
VARIABLE PLAYING STRATEGY

Lots of card counters have leaned how to keep track of the cards and bet their money according to the true count. However, not all that many go to the lengths of memorizing scores of index numbers for how to play their hands. Many just play all their hands according to basic strategy regardless of the count. It's already been mentioned that *betting* by the count is more important than *playing* by the count --- *but how much more important?* That depends upon the number of decks as well as the playing efficiency of your count system, and whether it's the *balanced* or *unbalanced* type.

209

Following are the results of four 200 million hand computer simulation runs using the *Mentor Count* in our model two deck game *(H17, DAS)*. The balanced *Mentor Count* has an excellent playing efficiency *(62%)*, and effectively implements a full range of 80 index numbers. Player performances are listed for 4 different modes of play. The betting spread when used, was 1-to-6 units with 2 units off the top.

MODE OF PLAY	RESULT	NET CHANGE
A) Basic Strategy with flat bets	-.42%	----
B) Mentor Variable Strategy with flat bets	-.25%	.17%
C) Mentor Count bets w/ basic strategy	+.45%	.87%
D) Mentor Count for betting and playing	+.82%	1.24%

With two decks, playing the hands with a full chart of index numbers was worth about .37% more than counting w/ just basic strategy for the hands. It's already been noted in other blackjack literature that most of that gain comes from using "the Illustrious 18" hands *(most of which are contained in the KISS index charts)*. The more index numbers you add, the less additional help you get.

Also, that gain will depend upon the playing efficiency of your particular count. Notice in the systems comparison chart on page 194 that the *Mentor Count* outperformed the *Hi/Lo Count* by .08% in the two deck game. Yet, both have a 97% betting correlation where the *Mentor* is 62% for playing and the *Hi/lo* is 51%. Some backup computer runs showed that indeed, when simply betting by the count and playing all hands according to basic strategy, both count systems produced the same net gain.

Other systems such as the *Omega II* and the *Hi-Opt II* have even better playing efficiencies *(67%)*, and could likely reap another few hundredths percent from proper basic strategy departures. Both however, give up considerable betting accuracy due to ignoring the *Ace*. Used "as is", they fall a little short of most multi-level "*Ace* reckoned" counts, but perform superbly when used in conjunction with a separate side-count of *Aces* for bet sizing.

Further simulations indicated that with other decks, a full set of index numbers will outperform basic strategy by roughly the amounts shown on the next page *(when used with a typical betting spread)* .

210

w/ SINGLE DECK	.50%
w/ DOUBLE DECK	.35%
w/ FOUR DECKS	.25%
w/ SIX DECKS	.20%
w/ EIGHT DECKS	.15%

EPILOGUE

Well, that's the blackjack story. Now you know that casino *'21'* is a beatable game. You also know what it takes to beat it. On these pages you've been introduced to some plain and simple ways to gain the tiniest edge, and some complex ways to gain a more significant one. The list below summarizes your net edge or disadvantage depending upon your chosen strategy. All figures are quoted in round numbers against a six deck shoe with typical rules and $4^1/_4$ decks dealt out.

Straight Basic Strategy	-.50%
Basic w/ Mag 7 & Hand Interaction	-.20% avg.
Ace/10 Front Count	+.25%
Entry Level KISS Count	+.50%
Stage II KISS	+.65%
Stage III KISS	+.70%
Mentor Count	+.75%

Now pick out a strategy that's right for you and combine it with the "table savvy" traits mentioned in Chapter 11. The bottom five choices on the list will equip you to take on the casino at their own game, on their court and gain the upper hand. But I need to remind you one last time that although blackjack is definitely a beatable game, *winning at it is not a 100% sure thing. If Lady Luck doesn't like you, she can hold you back for a long time.* The good news is, the Lady doesn't live forever. With a medium strength system such as KISS II, there's roughly a 60% chance you'll be ahead of the game after 60 hours of play. That chance increases to 90% after 1200 hours and to 99% after 4000 hours at the tables.

Still, the final, *key* ingredient has to be your own personal determination. It'll take *unwavering discipline, steely cold nerves, a nonchalant table manner and plenty of backup loot.* You'll need to become that "scholar/hustler" spoken of on the previous pages of this book. That's the part that stops most players.

WILL IT STOP YOU???

Chapter 12
KEY POINTS

1) There are well over two dozen different "fully structured" card counting systems in use today. Some track as few as eight cards, each with a value of +/- one point -- while others count all the cards with a value of from one to three points each.

2) There is not a great deal of difference between the performances of a well designed single level count and a well designed level 3 count.

3) Most of any improvement from adding "levels" to a card count comes when upgrading from level 1 to level 2.

4) The *Mentor Count* is a top performing level 2 system that is on a par with most level 3 systems.

5) The *Mentor Count* requires converting to the "true count" for betting and playing the hand. A "quick-conversion" chart is enclosed to ease the process.

6) The Variable Playing Strategy charts contain about 80 index numbers to indicate when specific hands should be played differently from the basic strategy.

7) Using a complete variable playing strategy will improve a card counter's edge over basic strategy hand decisions by roughly .15% to .50% depending upon the number of decks used.

RECOMMENDED READING

There are about a zillion blackjack books out there. Some of them will lead you down the rosy path to oblivion with unrealistic promises and dead-end strategies. Others are quite realistic, instructional and helpful. Following is a list of books I've read which have helped me grow immeasurably as a blackjack player.

Blackbelt in Blackjack by Arnold Snyder, Cardoza Publishing
Originally written in 1983, then redone in 1998 and 2005, this "hands on" down-to-earth manual provides some of the best coverage of blackjack basics and advanced skills to be found anywhere. It contains a visually graphic definition of the "true count" concept and a detailed 25 page chapter on shuffle tracking. Three count systems; *the Red-7, Hi-Lo Lite* and the excellent *Zen Count* are featured.

Professional Blackjack by Stanford Wong, Pi Yee Press
Very strong in the technical aspects of the game. Wong provides correct strategies and player's expectations for virtually all rule and deck variations. Monster charts supply the percentages for every player's hand vs. dealer's up-card. Two pro-level card counts; the *Hi/Lo* and *Halves Count* are included in ultra-fine detail.

Theory of Blackjack by Peter Griffin, Huntington Press
Griffin supplies gobs of math-based blackjack theory. From his conceptual analyses are derived definitive evaluations of card count betting and playing effectiveness, relative costs of misplaying hands and extremely precise basic strategy packages for various rules/decks.

Playing Blackjack as a Business by Lawrence Revere, Lyle Stuart Publishing. Hailing from the early 70's, it has become a "bible" for *"21"* players. Its many multi-colored charts, generated by Julian Braun go a long way towards building your understanding of blackjack's innards.

Blackjack Attack by Don Schlesinger, RGE publishing
A terrific collection of truly important card counting situational considerations analyzed and quantified exquisitely by the author. Contains a gold mine of information.

213

Blackjack for Blood by Bryce Carlson, Huntington Press
First penned in 1994, then updated in 2017. A thorough operational handbook for the card counter. Includes lots of pro-level "tricks of the trade". Built around the *Omega II* — an excellent level two count for single & double deck, conveniently adaptable to multi-deck shoes.

Blackjack Essays by Mason Malmuth, 2+2 Publishing
Malmuth is a highly descriptive writer. For the ongoing blackjack player he analyzes scores of controversial blackjack topics in a clear and unbiased manner. Good for building your depth of understanding.

Best Blackjack by Frank Scoblete, Bonus Books
A "soup to nuts" coverage of the game in general depth from basic strategy, to card counting to playing for comps. Printed in 1996; an educational overview of 1990's blackjack and beyond.

Burning the Tables in Las Vegas by Ian Andersen, Huntington Press.
An enlightening and entertaining read on the many ways to conceal your card counting abilities. It covers the gambit from camouflage plays, to cover betting to disguises.

Get the Edge at Blackjack by John May, Bonus Books.
Mostly for hard core players. John May discusses several "outside the box" methods of gleaning an edge at the game. Some require team play and other methods are ethically debatable.

Knockout Blackjack by Ken Fuchs & Olaf Vancura, Huntington Press.
Probably the most popular blackjack book of the 1990's. Introduces the now famous *KO Count*, a very popular and capable unbalanced level one count system.

Golden Touch Blackjack Revolution by Frank Scoblete, Research Services Unlimited.
Written in 2006, presents the novel, simple and moderately effective *Speed Count*. It's not a traditional "plus/minus" count, but a tally of hands played vs. low cards played.

Blackjack; take the Money & Run by Henry Tamburin, Research Services Unlimited.
For the average casino goer, provides a rounded instructional approach to effective blackjack play.

Blackjack and the Law by I. Nelson Rose and Robert Loeb, RGE Publishing.
For serious players, it deals with the legalities of being barred, alias ID's, tax issues, internet gambling and card counting itself. A bevy of legal information.

Glossary of Blackjack Terms

Ace Side-count - keeping a separate track of the Aces that are played.

Anchor Seat - "3rd base"; last to act before the dealer.

Backcount - tracking the cards while observing a game in progress.

Balanced Count - count systems whose high + low cards total to zero.

Barring - permanently ejecting a player, often for counting cards.

Basic Strategy -optimum strategy without regard for the played cards.

Betting Spread - the ratio between a player's min. & max. bet.

Betting Correlation - a card count's ability to track the betting edge.

Borderline Hand - one in which the correct decision is very marginal.

Break the deck - shuffling prematurely, usually to thwart card counting.

Card Clumping - the belief that high cards tend to stick together & vise versa.

Card Counting - keeping track of the cards that have been played.

CSM's - shufflers that continuously shuffle the cards while in the shoe.

Even Money - taking insurance when you have blackjack.

First Base - the seat to the dealer's immediate left and first to act.

Flat Bet - betting the same amount on every hand.

Hard Hand - a hand containing an Ace counted as "1", or no Ace at all.

Head Up - playing alone against the dealer.

Heavy Board - an excess of 10-count cards on the board.

House Edge - mathematical advantage the casino has over the player.

Index Number -true count at which it becomes advantageous to play a hand differently from the basic strategy.

Insurance - betting that the dealer has a 10-card underneath her Ace.

Light Board - a deficiency of 10-count cards on the board.

Marker - playing off a credit line with the casino rather than on cash.

Mimic the Dealer - to play all your hands the same as the dealer.

Natural - a blackjack; "21" on the first two cards.

Never Bust Strategy - to never risk hitting a stiff hand (12 through16).

Paint - any picture card such as a Jack, Queen or King.

Pat - to stand and take no more cards.

Penetration - how far the deck is dealt out before the shuffle.

Playing Efficiency - a card count's accuracy at detecting when the basic strategy should be deviated from.

Progressive Betting - sizing your next bet according to the last result.

Push - a "tie", such as when both player and dealer have "18".

Running Count - an up-to-date tally of high vs. low played cards.

Shuffle Track - monitoring points in the pack where valuable cards lie.

Snapper - slang for a dealt blackjack.

Soft Hand - a hand containing an Ace counted as "11".

Stiff - a hard hand between 12 and 16 (inclusively).

Third Base - seat to the dealer's immediate right and last to act.

Toke - a tip for a dealer or cocktail waitress.

True Count - gauging the high-low ratio of the unplayed cards.

Unit - the minimum wager in a player's betting spread.

INDEX